THE
THIRD OIL
SHOCK

Décalcomanie
of Oil and Dollar

SEJUNE OH, CFA

ISBN: 1479180157

ISBN 13:   9781479180158

To my beautiful wife for her endless love and support
And special thanks to Jae K. Yoo for translation

[AUTHOR]

Sejune Oh, CFA, FRM

After graduating from Architectural Engineering, Sejune acquired an MBA from KAIST (Korea Advanced Institute of Science & Technology). He is working as a fund manager at a Korean asset management company, and is actively writing and conducting lectures.

E-mail: ohsejune@hotmail.com

Contents

Part 2: History Explained with Oil and Dollars

Part 3: The Third Oil Shock

FOREWORD

What will be the course of oil price in the future? We should be prepared for a third oil shock.

The oil price that rose to \$140 a barrel in 2008 plummeted after the Lehman Brothers crisis, and rebounded to one hundred dollars. As Tunisia's Jasmine Revolution spread across the Middle East and North Africa in 2011, the oil price rose because of the political unrest the antigovernment protests brought. In the first half of 2012, the Iranian Revolution also acted as a fear factor and put pressure on increasing the oil price. Afterward, financial crises emerged in European countries, especially Greece and Spain, and oil price became weak. How will the oil price change in the future?

Oil production is concentrated in a few certain countries. As some of these countries are politically and financially unstable, a problem often occurs from the supply side of oil. On the other hand, oil-consuming countries are geographically far away from these countries, and usually are highly dependent on oil.

Furthermore, some transportation routes occupy a high proportion of oil trade. If this is interlocked with production problems, the ripple effects will be great. For example, the Strait of Hormuz is located between Iran and Oman. If this strait is blocked, approximately 20 percent of worldwide oil trade will have a problem. The Strait of Malacca is located between Indonesia, Malaysia, and Singapore. This is an important gateway to Asia, and 15 percent of worldwide trades of oil are conducted through this route.

Like this, there exists an imbalance of oil supply and demand. The psychological influence that alternative energy sources, such as nuclear energy, have on oil price can't be ignored. In March of 2011, an accident occurred in which radiation leaked from the Fukushima nuclear power plant because of an earthquake in Japan. Afterward, animosity toward nuclear power plants built up and movement against nuclear power plants occurred. As alternative energies, such as solar and wind, aren't yet efficient, breaking away from the efficient nuclear power may result in an increase in oil dependence. And if the oil price becomes unstable, it could have the effect of eliminating the upper limit.

Most books on oil seem to have been written by people who have worked or still work in the oil industry. Writings of scholars or journalists in the related fields can be seen every now and then. As a fund manager, I would like to interpret the past, considering both the oil and the dollar through the eyes of a financier, and suggest a new point of view. I will look at the interests of each country and reinterpret the history of oil and the dollar with the Oil-Dollar Composite Index.

In Part 1, the process how the oil majors developed through competition and cooperation, and the oil-producing countries' acknowledgment of their own power, will be dealt with. Beginning with the rise of the US in the Middle East, nationalism emerged in the oil-producing countries, and power shifted from the oil majors to the oil-producing countries, which appeared as a result in the first and second oil shock.

In Part 2, history will be reinterpreted considering both oil and the dollar. The past will be inspected with the Oil-Dollar Composite Index, and the dollar's role will be reilluminated in the interpretation of the history of oil. The winners and losers of the oil shock followed by the dollar shock will be shown.

In Part 3, the oil price is understood not through supply and demand, but through the interests and balance of power of the countries. If we can understand the pending issues with the wisdom gained in Part 1 and Part 2, we can predict the direction of the oil price.

I hope that the readers gain wisdom from this book.

Sejune Oh, CFA, FRM

Part 1

Oil as a Resource
History of the Oligopoly

Era of the International Oil Company (IOC)

Preview

Oil companies learn the benefits of cooperation through competition.

Summary

From the beginning of the oil industry, it seems that the word *monopoly* cannot be separated from it. This is true up to the point that it is enough to use only words that represent monopoly, such as Rockefeller (John D. Rockefeller), Seven Sisters, and OPEC (Organization of the Petroleum Exporting Countries), to describe the history of the oil industry. The major oil companies developed as they competed and cooperated while representing the interest of their countries. Especially during WWI and WWII, securing oil became a major issue of national security. During this time, the United States seized the opportunity by starting from the Arabian Peninsula, which was preoccupied by the United Kingdom.

Birth of the Oil Majors

The development of the United States' oil industry began with Edwin Drake finding oil at Titusville, Pennsylvania, in 1859. John Davison Rockefeller, who started an oil refinery company in the state of Ohio in 1863, experienced a plunge in oil price due to periodic oversupply and found out about the importance of controlling the supply. In 1870, Rockefeller founded Standard Oil and focused on suppressing competition by seizing control over oil refining and transportation (railways, pipelines, tankers) instead of production. At the time, even within the United States, oil production was hard to monopolize. This is because, first of all, there were numerous companies tackling the vast land. And second, it was risky in that even while using costly excavations, there was no guarantee that an oilfield would be found. This made it impossible even for Rockefeller to dominate the market. On the other hand, there were a relatively small number of companies in the refining and transportation business. Rockefeller gained price competitiveness through favorable freight expenses by primarily controlling the railways. After gaining price competitiveness, he either aggressively acquired his competitors or made them go bankrupt through price competition. By the early 1880s, the company took control over 80 to 90 percent of the US oil-refining industry and also dominated the oil pipeline and tanker industries. Then Rockefeller bought oilfields and achieved vertical integration. In 1882, Standard Oil Trust was established to control subsidiaries in the US, and by the mid-1880s, 70 percent of sales occurred through exports all over the world.

Even with the domination of the oil industry, Rockefeller's Standard Oil went under fire. With oilfields being found near Spindletop, Texas in 1901 and Tulsa, Oklahoma in 1905, competitors sprang up within the US. In addition to this, in international markets, Royal Dutch Shell emerged as a competitor. However, the real hardship began with the Sherman Antitrust Act enacted in 1890. After several years of trial, in 1911 the Supreme Court adjudicated for Standard Oil to be dismantled into more than thirty independent companies.

Standard Oil of New Jersey, also known as ESSO, which acted as the holding company of Standard Oil, later on became Exxon. In 1999, Exxon acquired Mobil and became ExxonMobil.

Standard Oil of New York, also known as Socony, later on became Mobil. At the time, Exxon and Mobil had vast distribution networks across the world. However, because they barely had any crude oil, they entered the international markets aggressively.

Standard Oil of California, also known as Socal, later on became Chevron. In 1985, they acquired Gulf Oil, and in 2001, they acquired Texaco. Unlike Exxon and Mobil, Chevron developed as a company that focuses on oil production.

After Rockefeller's Standard Oil was expelled due to violating antitrust laws, Gulf Oil and Texaco developed in the state of Texas. Gulf Oil started in 1901 with the discovery of oil at Spindletop, Texas. Later on, Gulf Oil expanded internationally and became a major company.

Texas Fuel Company also started in 1901 with the discovery of oil at Spindletop. Texas Fuel Company later on became Texaco and created the joint venture Caltex with Chevron.

These five companies (although now they have been incorporated into two companies), plus Royal Dutch Shell and BP (European companies will be introduced next) were called the Seven Sisters. Until OPEC's influence increased in the 1970s, the Seven Sisters had absolute power over the oil industry.

In 1907, Royal Dutch Shell was born with the merging of Royal Dutch (Netherlands) and Shell (United Kingdom) with an ownership of sixty to forty, respectively. Marcus Samuel, founder of Shell, was well aware of the importance of distribution. Samuel, who had control over Russian crude oil, shipped oil to the Far East on oil tankers that went through the Suez Canal. Shell started to compete against Rockefeller's Standard Oil, which dominated the Asian market at that time. Royal

Dutch was founded by Jean Kessler and merged with Shell, by Henri Deterding, due to hardship the company experienced because of the lack of crude oil.

William Knox D'Arcy won mining concessions from Iran in 1901, discovered oil in 1908, and established Anglo-Persian Oil Company in 1909. Stable oil procurement became important after the British Navy switched their fuel from coal to oil. Accordingly, the British government acquired a 51 percent stake in Anglo-Persian Oil Company and nationalized it. In 1935, the company was renamed Anglo-Iranian Oil Company, which changed to British Petroleum, and then became BP in 2001.

From Competition to Cooperation

The world's first mass-produced car, Ford's Model T, was first produced in 1908. The conveyor system was introduced in 1913, and up until Model T was discontinued in 1927, fifteen million units were manufactured. Before World War I broke out in 1914, coal was the main raw material for warships, while oil was only beginning to be used as raw material for warships.

Through World War I, countries came to understand that securing oil—which was the raw material for tanks, warships, and aircrafts—could determine the fate of war. After the war ended, the Ottoman Empire, which had vast oil reserves, was divided between the UK and France. The Ottoman Empire, which was defeated in World War I, lost most of its territories such as Arabia and North Africa, and was limited to the territory that is now Turkey. In April of 1920, it was decided at the San Remo Conference that Iraq and Palestine would go under the mandate of the UK, and that Lebanon, and Syria would go under the mandate of France. These matters were concluded with the Treaty of Sèvres in August of 1920.

At the San Remo Conference, the problem of how the shares of the Turkish Petroleum Company (TPC) should be divided emerged as a major issue. The Turkish Petroleum Company was established to attain oil concession for the area of Mesopotamia, which is now Iraq. BP owned 50 percent of the shares, while Shell and Deutsche Bank each had 22.5 percent, and Calouste Gulbenkian, which was an Armenian businessman, had 5 percent. Because Germany was defeated, Germany's shares went to France as war reparations. However, the US opposed to this and made an appeal. The US demanded for a portion of the share, pointing out the contribution they had made to the victory of the Allied Forces. After years of discussion, in July of 1928, they came to an agreement that BP, Royal Dutch Shell, the five US companies (later on, except Exxon and Mobil, the American companies withdrew.), and CFP, a French oil company (which is now Total SA) each own 23.75 percent and Gulbenkian own 5 percent of the shares. These companies agreed not to compete within the territory of the former Ottoman Empire (Iraq, Saudi Arabia, Bahrain, etc.) and marked the area with a red line which is known as the famous Red Line Agreement. This represented the beginning of the oil cartel. Iraq asked for a 20 percent share of the Turkish Petroleum Company at the San Remo Conference, but was rejected by the oil majors. Oil-producing countries only started participating in controlling oil production in the 1970s. Afterwards, nationalization was gradually introduced.

In September of 1928, Walter Teagle of Exxon, Henri Deterding of Royal Dutch Shell, and John Cadman of BP got together at Achnacarry Castle located in Scotland and reached an agreement called the Achnacarry Agreement or the As-Is Agreement. In the agreement, they set a production quota so that they can prevent the plunge of the crude oil price due to overproduction from excessive competition. This actually divided the global market among them. Later on, all the other oil majors were affected by this principle.

In 1929, the Great Depression occurred in the US and the demand for oil reduced. And in 1930, a large oilfield was discovered in the east part of Texas creating an oversupply of oil. These two together brought a crisis to the oil industry. At the time, the Railroad Commission of Texas, a state agency, allocated the amount of oil to the oil producers and restricted the supply, which had the oil price recover starting from 1935. Afterwards, the Railroad Commission of Texas posed a huge influence on the production and price of oil in the US and showed the importance of controlling oil supplies. Later on, this became the model for the oil-producing countries' cartel, OPEC.

In 1932, Shell and BP created a joint venture "Shell-Mex and BP" to suppress competition in the UK. In the UK, these two companies sold through this joint venture. The joint venture was a successful business until 1976 when it was dismantled.

However, unfortunately, the collaboration of the oil majors resulted in certain countries being pressured. The oil majors sealed off Mexico's oil when the president of Mexico, Lázaro Cárdenas, nationalized the oil companies in 1938. In 1951, the oil majors sealed off Iran's oil due to nationalization of oil companies and imposed an economic blow. These events isolated the two countries and showed that the oil majors had absolute power over oil-producing countries. Afterwards, the cases of Mexico and Iran were used as examples, which empowered the oil majors, when negotiating with oil-producing countries. Without the cooperation of the oil majors which secured refining, transportation, and sales networks of oil, oil-producing countries became isolated. This was rooted in Rockefeller's lessons.

However, by the 1970s, the power started to shift from the oil majors to the oil-producing countries. This happened after Libya succeeded in raising the posted price and tax rate which helped the oil-producing countries by increasing the income from the oil majors.

US's Successful Expansion in the Middle East

Thanks to the contribution they made during World War I, the US successfully gained the right to join in on the oil benefits sought from the Middle East. The US oil companies succeeded in gaining 23.75 percent shares of Turkish Petroleum Company (TPC) and started building up presence in the Middle East. On the other hand, this also meant the weakening of UK's control over the Middle East. In fact, BP had 50 percent of TPC's shares, but was reduced to 23.75 percent due to the US and France cutting in. Later on, UK's BP made one of the biggest mistakes in history by misjudging that there would be no oil in Arabia, which then resulted in handing over the hegemony of oil to the US.

First, let's go over some history. UK's dominance in the Arabian Peninsula used to be absolute. Bahrain was a protectorate of UK from 1880 to 1971, and Kuwait was a colony of the UK from 1899 to 1961. Therefore, UK was very influential over Bahrain and Kuwait, which meant that oil concessions were only given with consent from the UK.

Saudi Arabia was under UK's rule after their independence from the Ottoman Empire in 1922 until 1927. In 1932, Saudi Arabia became independent and was named the current country by King Ibn Saud. Because BP made a big misjudgment in predicting that there will be no oil in Saudi Arabia, the UK government made a mistake of not considering Saudi Arabia as an important country. As Saudi Arabia became independent earlier than the other countries under UK's rule, the US gained an opportunity to become influential.

Another thing that helped UK's dominance over the Middle East was the Red Line Agreement, which was mentioned above. The members of the Turkish Petroleum Company, which became Iraq Petroleum Company (IPC) in 1929, that signed the Red Line Agreement could not independently pursue control over oil in the Middle East. This made it difficult for the US to gain dominance in the Middle East.

Changes started to occur after a New Zealander named Frank Holmes gained oil concessions in Bahrain, Kuwait, and Saudi Arabia. Later on, he lost oil concessions to Saudi Arabia, but sold Bahrain and Kuwait's oil concessions to a US company called Gulf. Since it was part of the Ottoman Empire, Bahrain was a country that was applied to the Red Line Agreement. Therefore, Gulf could not independently develop oil. However, BP was not interested in Bahrain. So Gulf sold its oil concession in Bahrain to another US oil company named Socal, which was not a member of the Red Line Agreement. The event of oil concessions of Bahrain (which was a protectorate of the UK) being handed over to a US oil company stirred a diplomatic reaction. This dispute was solved by Gulf selling the rights to

Socal (now Chevron), which was a company located in Canada, a British Commonwealth country. Oilfields were discovered in Bahrain in 1931, which then increased the hope of finding other oilfields in the Arabian Peninsula.

Meanwhile, unlike Bahrain, Kuwait was not part of the Red Line Agreement. So Gulf maintained the oil concessions. However, since Kuwait was under UK's rule, Gulf had to establish a joint venture with BP. Both companies had 50 percent share in the new joint venture Kuwait Oil Company. In 1938, a large-scale oilfield, the Burgan Field was found, and full-scale production started in 1946. Due to the Burgan Field, Kuwait emerged as a major oil country. However, in 1991 as the Gulf War broke out, part of the Burgan Fields was burned by the Iraqi army.

The western countries were not interested in Saudi Arabia because they thought the country had no oil. In 1933, Socal, which first advanced into Bahrain, obtained oil concessions in Saudi Arabia. However, Socal did not have enough funding nor sales channels to establish the infrastructure to produce and transfer the oil. In 1936, Texaco, which was not part of the Red Line Agreement, attained 50 percent shares of Socal. This joint venture's name was changed to Aramco (Arabian American Oil Company) in 1944.

With the outbreak of World War II in 1939, Socal and Texaco required protection by the US government with their business in Saudi Arabia. President Franklin D. Roosevelt acknowledged the importance of securing oil outside the US and had the US government intervene in Saudi Arabia affairs. This modeled the intervention the UK had on Iranian oil. Exxon and Mobil also acknowledged the importance of Saudi Arabia's oil and tried to cancel the Red Line Agreement. Exxon and Mobil suggested a way to increase profits to the partners (BP, Shell, CFP, and Gulbenkian) of the Red Line Agreement, and were able to cancel it in 1948. At first Exxon and Mobil were suggested 20 percent of Aramco's shares. However, Mobil only took 10 percent shares. In the end, Exxon took 30 percent, Mobil 10 percent, Socal 30 percent, and Texaco 30 percent shares of Aramco. These four US oil companies took over Saudi Arabia's oil and the US became an influential country in the Middle East oil market. The Trans-Arabian Pipeline began construction in 1947 and started transporting Saudi Arabia's oil to Sidon, Lebanon in 1949. This pipeline acted as a big part of global oil trade.

During the movement of oil-producing countries increasing shares in the 1970s, Saudi Arabia gradually increased their shares in Aramco. After the US helped Israel in the Yom Kippur War (Fourth Arab-Israeli War) in 1973, Saudi Arabia took 25 percent shares of Aramco. In 1974, they gained 60 percent, and in 1980, they finally gained 100 percent shares of Aramco. So in 1988, Aramco became Saudi Arabia's national oil company Saudi Aramco.

Conclusions

The rise of the US in the Middle East was probably not only due to the UK's misjudgments of oil in the Arabian Peninsula, but also due to US's rise in national power. The US entered the Middle East market by attaining shares in the Turkish Oil Company for contributing to the victory of the Allied Forces. The US was able to maintain oil concessions even in Bahrain and Kuwait, which was under absolute control by the UK, because of their growing influence. As World War II came to an end in 1944, the US dollar replaced the British pound as the reserve currency for the Bretton Woods system. This showed that the US became the most powerful country in the world. It is probably not a coincidence that the US oil companies dominated one of the largest oilfields, Saudi Arabia.

In 1919, Woodrow Wilson (the twenty-eighth US president) advocated the National Self Determination at the Paris Peace Conference, composed of the victor countries of World War I. The contents of this suggested that each nation has the right to decide their own fate, and other countries should not interfere. This gave hope to the many powerless countries that wanted to become independent, and in fact, influenced their actual independence. However, another beneficiary seemed to be the US. The UK and France started to accept the independence of their numerous colonies, which used to provide mass resources, and lost their vested rights. This made it easier for the US to access resources from these independent countries.

Rise of Nationalism and Emergence of New Competitors

Preview

As nationalism emerged, countries began using oil as a weapon. New competitors emerged and started to encroach on the existing oil cartel.

Summary

The oil majors retaliated to Mexico's effort of nationalizing oil in 1938. In 1951, Iran also suffered an economic hardship due to the oil majors boycotting oil for nationalizing their oil. However, the success of the Hydrocarbons Law (fifty-fifty split of profits between government and companies), set at Venezuela and legalized in 1948, spread to the Middle East and helped the oil-producing countries gain power. In 1960, the cartel OPEC, made by the oil-producing countries, was born. At first, after the formation of OPEC, the oil-producing countries did not cooperate with each other. However, later on, OPEC acknowledged its power and began writing its history.

France's CFP (now Total) and Italia's ENI (led by Enrico Mattei) emerged, and, starting in Libya, independent companies like Occidental Petroleum began to stand out.

Rise of Nationalism

Nationalism first emerged in Mexico, Latin America. While Mexico was under the ruling of Porfirio Diaz, Weetman Pearson (British) signed a civil engineering contract and created a relationship with Mexico. In 1909, he established the Mexican Eagle Oil Company, and in 1910 found a huge oilfield. However, in 1910, the Mexican Revolution occurred, and in the revision of constitutional law in 1917, the government claimed to own the oil. This became the basis for the nationalization of Mexican oil in 1938.

In 1919, Weetman Pearson sold Mexican Eagle Oil Company to Royal Dutch Shell. However, in 1938, President Lázaro Cárdenas nationalized the company and established it as the national oil company, Pemex. The oil majors succeeded in showing their power by boycotting Mexican oil in retaliation, but were unable to stop the movement of nationalization spreading to Venezuela and the Middle East.

Venezuela became independent in 1830 after approximately three hundred years of reigning by Spain. In 1908, oil concessions were handed over to overseas oil companies during Juan Vicente Gómez's rule over Venezuela. From 1914 to 1917, many oil fields were found and the oil majors crowded in. In 1929, Venezuela became the second largest oil-producing country after the US, and the world's largest oil exporter.

As Juan Pablo Pérez Alfonso, who founded OPEC, became the oil minister, he demanded a fifty-fifty distribution of profits (fifty-fifty formula) to the oil majors. The oil majors desperately opposed this. However, the law of dividing the profits by fifty-fifty was passed in 1948. This was the first real victory the oil-producing countries had over the oil majors. This was an event that announced the forthcoming relationship change between the two. Moreover, Venezuela became the first country out of the oil-producing countries to use the posted price, which was the standard for taxes. Although most of the time the market price was lower than the posted price, oil companies reluctantly had to pay according to the posted price.

After Saudi Arabia's king Ibn Saud heard of the Venezuela fifty-fifty profit sharing news, he immediately demanded this rule to be applied to Aramco. In 1950, following Venezuela, the oil majors had to concede in Saudi Arabia, too. Third-party oil companies from the US entered Saudi Arabia by paying more than Aramco for oil concessions which disrupted the proprietary system. Details about this part will come later. In addition, the US government prevented the advance of communism in the Middle East. They had no intentions to displease Saudi Arabia so that they could improve relations with them. The US government exempted taxes to the amount of additional pay the oil companies had to cover. Oil companies tried to maximize the effect of these tax exemptions by profit maximizing in upstream businesses like production, and minimizing in downstream activities such as transportation, refining, and sales.

As a result, the US government actually aided the oil companies. The US government also delegated some part of Middle East policy to the oil companies. In other words, the extra money oil companies paid to Saudi Arabia came from tax exemptions, which meant that taxes US citizens paid were used to sustain the oil companies' profits and aid Saudi Arabia. Because the US government officially supported Israel, they used their native oil companies to control the Middle East oil-producing countries, which were obviously hostile to Israel. Due to this duality, conflict was expressed through four Middle East wars, since the founding of Israel in 1948 to the first oil shock in 1973.

Black Tears of Iran

In 1925, RezāShāh dethroned Ahmad ShāhQājār and established the Pahlavi Dynasty. RezāShāh made a major contribution by constructing roads and railways, and in 1935 changed the country name from Persia to Iran. He also put his efforts in trying to create a better oil contract with Anglo-Persian Oil Company, which is now BP. As World War II broke out and the Nazis (Germany) invaded the Soviet Union (Russia) in 1939, the UK and the Soviet Union invaded Iran in 1941 to secure oil. In 1941, RezāShāh was dethroned by the UK because he was favorable to the Nazis. After being dethroned, he wandered foreign countries until he died in 1944.

The UK seated RezāShāh's son Mohammad RezāShāhon the throne at the age of twenty-two. After the war, nationalism emerged in Iran. Iran demanded that the fifty-fifty rule of Venezuela be applied to their country. However, BP rejected. In 1951, Prime Minister Haj-Ali Razmara, who supported BP, was assassinated, and Mohammad Mosaddegh who argued the nationalization of oil, became the prime minister and carried out his claim. However, just like Mexico, the Iranian economy suffered a downfall due to the oil major's boycott.

In 1953, the US and the UK led a coup, brought down Mohammad Mosaddegh, and brought back Mohammad RezāShāh to Iran. The reason why the US was involved is unclear. However, shortly after the coup, they received ample compensations. As a new consortium was established in Iran in 1954, the market that was once dominated by BP was split among the oil majors. BP took 40 percent, the five major US oil companies (Exxon, Mobil, Texaco, Gulf, and Chevron) each took 8 percent, Royal Dutch Shell took 14 percent, and CFP

(Total) took 6 percent of the shares. In 1955, the independent US oil companies took part in the Iran-Consortium. The five major US oil companies dropped their share to 7 percent, which left 5 percent share to be divided among the nine independent US oil companies.

The independent US oil companies, which had political influence in the US, began penetrating the offshore markets of the oil majors. In addition, they protected their domestic market by asking the US government to limit the oil majors from importing cheap Middle East and Latin American oil. In terms of energy security, the US government probably could not let the oil majors import cheap Middle East oil and bankrupt the independent oil companies. It was the US government that actually helped the independent oil companies to secure a seat in the Iran-Consortium. This helped the independent oil companies to safely enter international markets. As a result, new competitors emerged that eroded the Seven Sisters' markets.

New Competitors

Jean Paul Getty, who was from Minneapolis, made big money by operating oil rigs in Oklahoma. Afterward, he acquired Tidewater Oil and Skelly Oil. In 1949, Jean Paul Getty suggested to King Ibn Saud that he would pay a higher fee than the oil majors currently paid. This suggestion let him gain oil concessions in Saudi Arabia. In 1953, he discovered an oil field and became one of the wealthiest people in the world. As the independent oil companies rushed into the Middle East, the oligopoly of the Seven Sisters withered. In 1954, Getty Oil was absorbed by Texaco.

The independent oil companies particularly stood out in Libya. Nelson Bunker Hunt, son of oil tycoon H. L. Hunt, was successful in Libya. Libyan oil was competitively priced because the production costs were low, the quality was good due to low rate of sulfur, and the country was close to Europe. Therefore, Libyan oil helped the independent oil companies compete against the oil majors. Nelson Bunker Hunt is also famous for jumping in to silver speculation with his brother, William Herbert Hunt, and going bankrupt in 1988, after silver prices collapsed in 1980.

Occidental Petroleum, ran by Armand Hammer, operated in Libya since 1965, and also entered Oman and Columbia.

As mentioned above, the nine independent US oil companies took part of the oil majors' share in Iran and gained a large amount of benefits without any big risks.

Other than the independent oil companies, Italy's national oil company ENI, ran by Enrico Mattei, gave the Seven Sisters a hard time by breaking the existing rules. The name "Seven Sisters" was coined by Enrico Mattei. During World War II, he acted as part of the Italian resistance movement, and in 1945, he took the task of dismantling the national oil company AGIP (Azienda Generale Italiana Petroli), which was established during the fascist regime. However, rather than dismantling the company, he reorganized and developed it by finding oil and gas, and he made a significant contribution to the economic development of Italy. In 1953, he established national oil company ENI (Ente Nazionale Idrocarburi). In 1954, he wanted to join the Iran-Consortium but was excluded by the oil majors. In 1957, when Enrico Mattei got another opportunity in Iran, rather than the normal fifty-fifty rule, he gave Iran 75 percent of the profits and took only 25 percent. This showed how much the oil majors exploited the oil-producing countries, which came as a big blow to the oil majors. In addition, Libya was given a similar offer.

In the late 1950s, ENI changed the course of history by waging a price war with the oil majors by supplying cheap Russian oil to Europe. Due to competition, the market price of oil continuously dropped. Because the agreed posted price with the oil-producing countries was fixed, the oil companies had to take the differences as losses. So, the oil majors reduced costs by cutting down the posted price in 1959 and 1960 by force. Because of this, tax revenues were reduced in oil-producing countries, and this enraged them. In this way, Enrico Mattei's ENI made the oil-producing countries aware of the fact that the oil majors were making undue profits. By using Russia's cheap oil, ENI waged a price war and eventually had the posted price drop. This in turn enraged the oil-producing countries and had them unite, and this triggered the birth of OPEC. In September of 1960, a month after the second reduction in the posted price, OPEC was formed. Enrico Mattei, who shook the international oil market, unfortunately died in a plane crash in 1962.

Birth of Another Cartel, OPEC

In the late 1950s, large oil fields were found in the Middle East and Africa, and Russia increased oil exports, which resulted in an oversupply of oil. The oil-producing countries were furious when the oil majors reduced the posted price. So in September of 1960, at the invitation of Iraq, representatives of the five countries Iran, Kuwait, Saudi Arabia, Venezuela, and Iraq gathered at Baghdad and established a cartel for the oil-producing countries, OPEC (Organization of Petroleum Exporting Countries). As of 2012, there were twelve members of OPEC which include four countries from Africa (Algeria, Angola, Nigeria, & Libya), two countries from Latin America (Venezuela & Ecuador), and six countries from the Middle East (Iran, Iraq, Kuwait, Saudi Arabia, Qatar, & United Arab Emirates).

The oil-producing countries were able to stop additional drops in the posted price, but were unable to come to an agreement on production regulations and oil prices. Saudi Arabia and Iran had conflict over the OPEC initiative, which showed that they were not truly united. Moreover, the oil-producing countries could not take full control over the oil companies because they still dominated oil-producing technology, transportation, and sales. Furthermore, although each oil-producing country wanted to increase tax revenues from oil by increasing the production, the oil companies limited the amount of oil produced in each country to prevent oversupply.

The reason OPEC's influence was limited in the 1960s was not only because the countries had conflict in interests, but also because of the oversupply of oil. In the 1960s Libya, Nigeria, Algeria, and Egypt found oil fields, and Africa's oil production skyrocketed.

Of course, the interests of the oil majors were also not fully aligned. Mobil needed more oil because they only had 10 percent shares compared to 30 percent shares Exxon, Texaco, and Socal had in Saudi Arabia's Aramco. It was also obvious at the Iran-Consortium that France's newborn Total and the Seven Sisters (which had sufficient sources for oil) were in different positions. On one hand, there were some oil companies that could tame the oil-producing countries and control the price of oil with sufficient oil supplies, whereas, on the other hand, there were oil companies suffering from insufficient oil supplies. Due to the difference of opinions on the amount of oil production, conflict was inevitable.

Conclusions

In 1954, when the Iran-Consortium was founded, France's CFP took 6 percent of the shares and entered the Seven Sisters' territory. In 1955, nine independent US oil companies entered the consortium, dividing 5 percent shares among themselves. The Iran-Consortium's share composition best implies the collapse of the Seven Sisters' stronghold.

Afterward, activities of the independent oil companies ran by Getty, Hunt, Hammer, and so forth discomforted the Seven Sisters. These activities eventually helped the oil-producing countries gain bargaining powers. Enrico Mattei's activities were particularly impressive. Combined with the rise of nationalism, OPEC, a cartel to face the oil major's cartel, was founded in 1960.

Lessons from the Arab-Israeli War

Preview

Although the Arab countries lost to Israel in all four Arab-Israeli Wars from 1948 to 1973, they learned a lesson and acknowledged the power of oil. In the 1970s, they wrote the history of oil.

Summary

In 1948, with the help of the US, Israel established a country on favorable terms in Palestinian territory. In reaction, the Arab countries that opposed to this decision began the First Arab-Israeli War. The Arab countries lost to Israel, who was aided by the US, and were deprived part of their land. The Palestine refugee problem occurred as the Arabs were thrown out of their land. In 1956, the Second Arab-Israeli War occurred due to Egypt trying to nationalize the Suez Canal; and in 1967, the Third Arab-Israeli War occurred with Israel occupying territory of Jordan, Syria, and Egypt. The Arab countries attempted to weaponize oil, but failed. In 1973, the Fourth Arab-Israeli War occurred with Egypt and Syria attacking Israel to restore their territory. The oil-producing countries of the Middle East succeeded in weaponizing oil by uniting and banning exportation of oil to countries that supported Israel.

Afterward, there were numerous occasions when Israel and the Arabs tried to reconcile their dispute. However, even now, solving the problem between Israel and the Arabs seems remote.

The Birth of Israel, and the First Arab-Israeli War

The history of oil cannot be told without the history of conflict between Israel and the Arabs. The kingdom of Israel was founded in the eleventh century BC, but was destroyed by the Assyrians in the eighth century BC. The Israelis reestablished their country, but was once again defeated by the Romans in the first century, and then scattered around Europe. Zionism is a form of Jewish nationalism that supports the scattered and persecuted Jews who are rebuilding the country of Israel on their ancestors' land, Palestine.

During World War I, which broke out in 1914, the British brought in the Jews and Arabs to fight against the Ottoman Empire, offering them their independence. In 1915, the British made a secret agreement, the McMahon-Hussein

Correspondence, with the Arabs promising their independence in the Arab region, including Palestine. Meanwhile, in 1917, the British also made a secret agreement with the Jews called the Balfour Declaration that promised them the establishment of their country in the land of Palestine. The UK promised both the Jews and the Arabs the land of Palestine, and this brought about conflict between the two.

This was not the end. In 1916, the UK, France, and Russia got together and made the Sykes-Picot Agreement, which was about dividing the territories of the Ottoman Empire (including Palestine) among themselves. In 1920, the UK made a lot of promises they could not keep and was appointed to rule Palestine at the San Remo Conference. The Arabs became furious, and the anti-British sentiment reached its peak. Meanwhile, there was a surge in immigration because the Jews that were persecuted in Europe moved to Palestine. The conflict between the Jews and the original occupants, the Arabs, heightened, and in the late 1930s the Great Arab Revolt occurred.

After World War II, which lasted from 1939 to 1945, in February of 1947, the UK announced their withdrawal from Palestine, and delegated the Palestine problem to the UN. On November 29 of 1947, Palestine was divided into two countries at the UN general assembly. The US led this assembly that resulted in favorable results to the Jews. The Arabs who occupied the Palestine territory for more than two thousand years lost 56 percent of their territory to the Jews, who were only 33 percent of the population. The Arabs became outraged and the anti-American sentiment heightened. On May 14 of 1948, Israel declared independence. The very next day, Egypt, Iraq, Jordan, Syria, and Lebanon attacked Israel and started the First Arab-Israeli War. At first, the Arabs had the upper hand. However, with the help from the US, Israel took over 80 percent of Palestine territory and was the de facto winner. Israel's territory increased up until the Third Arab-Israeli War that occurred in 1967. The gradually decreasing territory for the Arabs created the Palestinian refugee problem, which emerged as an international concern.

Thus, by looking at the history before and after the First Arab-Israeli War, we may understand why nationalism emerged in the Middle East as well as how deep-rooted the anti-British and anti-American sentiments are. Because of the strong anti-British and anti-American sentiments and because they needed to obtain oil from the Middle East, the US and the UK had to delegate some of their political roles to multinational companies, such as the oil majors. The US especially had no other choice because they were officially supporting Israel. The US had no other choice but to loosen antitrust regulations for the oil majors, which brought in oil from hostile countries.

Nationalization of the Suez Canal, and the 2ⁿᵈ Arab-Israeli War

The Suez Canal has had a huge role in Egypt's oil history. The Suez Canal started construction in 1859 and was opened in 1869. It is a canal that connects the Mediterranean Sea, Red Sea, and the Indian Ocean, an important route that connects Europe and Asia. In particular, oil transportation was huge. If the Suez Canal could not be used, then Middle East oil had to be transported by going all around Africa. France and Egypt were once the major shareholders of the Suez Canal. However, after Egypt experienced financial difficulties in 1875, they sold their share to the UK, so the UK and France became the major shareholders. In 1882, when a riot occurred in Egypt, the UK took over Egypt under the pretext of protecting the Suez Canal. The neighboring countries were worried that the UK would abuse the use of the Suez Canal. So in 1888, nine countries, the UK, France, Germany, Hungary, the Ottoman Empire, Spain, Italy, the Netherlands, and Russia, got together at Constantinople and made the Convention of Constantinople that declared neutralization of the Suez Canal. However, even with the convention, the owners of the Suez Canal used it as a weapon whenever they needed to, such as the World War. Even after the independence in 1922, the UK had significant influence on Egypt. As of 2012, the Suez Canal is still occupied by the British military.

In 1952, Gamal Abdel Nasser orchestrated a coup d'etat and became the president of Egypt in 1954. Because Gamal Abdel Nasser introduced Russian weapons and was friendly to Russia, the US withdrew financial support for the construction of the Aswan Dam. In 1956, Gamal Abdel Nasser nationalized the Suez Canal to raise the necessary funds for the construction of the Aswan Dam by securing canal tolls. He also sealed off the route to the Gulf of Aqaba, which was a violation to the Convention of Constantinople.

For the UK and France, the Suez Canal was not only a major asset, but also an important route for transporting Middle East oil to Europe. The UK and France reacted to the nationalization of the Suez Canal with the military, and the Second Arab-Israeli War broke out. Israel conquered the Sinai Peninsula and the UK and France won the war by bombing Egypt. However, they had to withdraw their military and lose the Suez Canal because the US, Russia, and the UN put pressure on them. This event confirmed the powerful worldwide positions held by the US and Russia. This reflected the rise of the two countries and the decline of Europe.

Eventually, Gamal Abdel Nasser succeeded in nationalizing the Suez Canal and secured victory over British and French colonial forces and Israel. This also made him a hero of the Arabs. Tolls from the Suez Canal became a major source of income. Because blocking the Suez Canal limited the Middle East's oil supply to Europe, it was later used as a weapon.

Failure of Oil Weaponization and the Third Arab-Israeli War

When Israel was founded in 1948, a lot of Arabs who lived in Palestine were driven out of their land, and they became Palestinian refugees. When the Third Arab-Israeli War occurred in 1967, Israel took over a huge amount of Palestine territory, which left an additional hundreds of thousands of refugees. In 1964, the Palestine Liberation Organization (PLO) was organized to rebuild the Palestinian state and remove Israel. In 1967, after losing in the Third Arab-Israeli War, they expanded forces. In 1969, after Yasser Arafat became the chairman, PLO acted more aggressively and executed terrorist activities, which made it an international issue.

Israel had frequent disputes with its neighboring countries. Finally, on June 5 of 1967, Israel attacked Egypt, Syria, and Jordan, and won a complete victory in six days. This was known as the Six-Day War, the Third Arab-Israeli War. Thanks to this war, Israel conquered the vast territory of West Bank of Jordan, East Jerusalem, Golan Heights of Syria, the Sinai Peninsula, and the Gaza Strip of Egypt. The Suez Canal was closed by Egypt until June of 1975. In November of 1967, the United Nations Security Council Resolution 242, which contained a statement that the Israeli army would withdraw from conquered territories, was adopted, but eventually was not kept. On June 6, the very next day, the war broke out.

The Arab oil-producing countries imposed an oil embargo on the US and the UK. However, the US and the UK were not harmed at all because Iran and Venezuela did not join in on the oil embargo. The oil embargo only damaged the economy of the Arab countries that joined in.

Unable to unite on the oil embargo, and harming their own economy, the Arab oil-producing countries formed OAPEC (Organization of Arab Petroleum Exporting Countries) to discuss the political use of oil. OAPEC was formed in 1968 by Saudi Arabia, Libya, and Kuwait, and later on joined in by Algeria, Bahrain, United Arab Emirates, Qatar, Egypt, Iraq, and Syria.

The Fourth Arab-Israeli War and the Oil Shock

On October 6, 1973, Egypt and Syria led a surprise attack on Israel to regain territory that was lost during the previous wars. At first, it seemed like the Arabs would win. However, in the end, the Arabs lost again by an Israeli counterattack that was supported by the US This was the Fourth Arab-Israeli War, also known as the Yom Kippur War.

Meanwhile, OAPEC weaponized oil by banning oil exports to countries that cooperated with Israel. This time, it was much different from what happened during the Third Arab-Israeli War. In 1970, starting with Libya, oil-producing countries were on better terms when signing a contract with oil companies. In addition to this, nationalization of the oil industry progressed in each oil-producing country. So by 1973, the oil-producing countries' control on oil was at a level that couldn't even be slightly compared to the past. Even this time, Iran and Venezuela didn't join in on the oil embargo, but the Arabs were still successful in weaponizing oil. They brought the first oil shock. The oil price rose up approximately four times to twelve dollars per barrel. The world economy fell into a stagflation, an inflation of prices, and an economy recession. In 1979, due to the Iranian Revolution, oil workers went on a strike that disrupted the production of oil and resulted in the second oil shock.

Even though the two were at war, efforts of reconciliation between Israel and the Arabs did exist. In September of 1978, Jimmy Carter invited Egypt's president, Muhammad Anwar El Sadat, and Israel's prime minister, Menachem Begin, to the presidential retreat Camp David, and had them sign the Camp David Accords. This became the cornerstone for the Egypt-Israel Peace Treaty in March of 1979. In this treaty, Egypt became the First Arab country to accept Israel's existence, and the US promised Egypt financial and military support. Israel promised to return the Sinai Peninsula, conquered in 1967 during the Third Arab-Israeli War, and withdrew military forces in 1982. Muhammad Anwar El Sadat and Menachem Begin won the Nobel Peace Prize. However, Egypt was branded as a traitor and lost rights to the Arab League for some time. In the end, Muhammad Anwar El Sadat was assassinated in 1981.

The Palestine problem seemed to make progress as Israel and PLO signed the Oslo Accords. In this agreement, PLO acknowledged and stopped terrorism on Israel, and in return, Israel returned Gaza Strip and the West Bank of Jordan and acknowledged Palestinian authority. In 1994, Israel's prime minister, Yitzhak Rabin, and PLO's Yasser Arafat won the Nobel Peace Prize, but Yitzhak Rabin got assassinated in 1995.

In 2003, the US, Russia, and the EU (European Union) made the "Road Map for Middle East Peace," but it was never implemented.

Conclusions

Thus, by looking at the history of the Arab-Israeli conflict, we may understand the deep-rooted anti-British and anti-American sentiments. We may also assume the special role that the oil majors played to gain oil from the Arab countries that were hostile. The US indirectly supporting Saudi Arabia by giving tax cuts to oil companies for the amount of tax rises in Saudi Arabia may be a good example.

Looking at the big picture, the US accepted the independence of the oil-producing countries and created an environment for growth. The US slowly increased influence while having the influence of the European countries that dominated the Middle East, decline. This trend was more pronounced after the Suez Canal crisis, which can be seen as a confrontation between the US and Russia under the Cold War. The US financially supported the countries of Europe that fell into poverty and chaos after World War II through the Marshall Plan because they were afraid of the spread of communism. They helped reconstruct Europe, and succeeded in rooting democracy. The oil-producing countries' victory in the 1970s can be interpreted as the US indirectly supporting these countries in order to hold Russia in check.

Oil Shock

Preview

Through the first and second oil shocks, the oil-producing countries that attained control over oil production accomplished an economic leap. Even with a recession that occurred due to soaring oil prices, the oil majors' revenue and profits were at an all-time high because they still dominated oil production technology, transportation, and sales.

Summary

Muammar Gaddafi, who seized power in a coup in 1969, became a hero of the Arabs by increasing the oil price. He was able to do this by arguing that Libya's oil was of high quality and cheap to transport to Europe. In a meeting between the oil-producing countries and oil companies, the Tehran Agreement was signed on February 14, 1971. The agreement contained contents of raising the tax to 55 percent and increasing the posted price. Libya's success spread to the other oil-producing countries, and resulted in nationalization of oil assets. This increased control over oil production.

On October 6, 1973, the Fourth Arab-Israeli war broke out as Egypt and Syria attacked Israel in an attempt to recover land they lost in the past. The Arab countries weaponized oil by imposing an oil embargo to countries that supported Israel. This brought the first oil shock. As if reflecting the change in stature of the oil-producing countries, they were successful in weaponizing oil. The oil prices skyrocketed, which ended the era of cheap oil. At the end of 1978, the oil workers' strike of the Iranian Revolution led to a plunge in oil production and exports. This brought the second oil shock. In 1980, the Iran-Iraq War broke out and oil production rapidly decreased.

The oil price that remained at two to three dollars a barrel, increased to twelve dollars a barrel during the first oil shock, and exceeded forty dollars a barrel during the second oil shock. Due to soaring oil prices, the world experienced soaring commodity prices and economic recessions. Meanwhile, oil-producing countries accumulated vast wealth, and the oil majors achieved unprecedented performance.

Libya's Great Victory

Libya's oil had high quality and low production costs, and the country was geographically close to Europe, which made it an important supply for Europe. Libya's oil became even more important when the Suez Canal was closed. As Occidental Petroleum, led by Exxon and Dr. Armand Hammer, found large oilfields in Libya, it became prominent.

Gamal Abdel Nasser's ardent supporter Muammar Gaddafi seized control over Libya after a coup in 1969. He demanded a raise in taxes and the posted price of oil, arguing that Libya's oil quality was high and transportation to Europe was cheap. As always, the oil majors had other sources of oil supply, so they had nothing to lose by rejecting Muammar Gaddafi's demand. However, it was a different case for Occidental Petroleum because they were highly dependent on Libya's oil. Libya knew this, and demanded Occidental Petroleum to cut production. Occidental Petroleum yielded in September of 1970 and signed a new contract. Soon after, the other oil companies accepted the raise from 50 percent to 55 percent in taxes, and a raise in the posted price. This affected the contracts oil companies had with other countries. The time of the oil majors, which made Mexico and Iran give in by boycotting when they nationalized their oil, was over. Muammar Gaddafi led the great victory of Libya and became a hero of the Arabs.

On December of 1970, OPEC held a meeting at Caracas, Venezuela and passed a resolution that set the lowest tax rate to 55 percent and allowed changing the posted price according to changes in the exchange rate. Basic principles such as maximization of oil imports, equity participation in oil production, advances into oil refinery and sales, and protection of oil resources were also determined at this meeting. The victory of Libya spread to the oil-producing countries as the Tehran Agreement, which states an increase in taxes to 55 percent and an increase in the posted price, was signed at a meeting between the oil-producing countries and the oil companies.

The triumph of the oil-producing countries naturally led to a wave of equity participation. Algeria, which was a colony of France since 1830 to1962, was still under France's influence after their independence. However, in February of 1971, Algeria nationalized 51 percent shares of oil. Libya started nationalizing oil companies' assets in 1971 and Iraq nationalized Iraq Petroleum Company in 1972. Saudi Arabia gradually nationalized Aramco. In 1973, they acquired 25 percent shares, and in 1980, they acquired 100 percent shares. In 1988, the company became Saudi Aramco. In 1974, Kuwait and Nigeria nationalized oil assets, and in 1976, Venezuela followed. The nationalization of oil assets expanded the control over oil production by oil-producing countries.

The First Oil Shock

The Fourth Arab-Israeli War, when Egypt and Syria attacked Israel on October 6, 1973, was the root of the first oil shock. As the US once again supported Israel in this war, OPEC announced the oil price as $5.1 a barrel (a 70 percent increase) on October 16. On October 17, the ministers of OAPEC got together and weaponized oil by agreeing on cutting oil production 5 percent a month until Israel withdrew forces from conquered territories. The Arab countries imposed an oil embargo on Israel-friendly countries, such as the US and the Netherlands. The oil embargo contributed to the rise in oil prices, which hit $11.65 a barrel on January of 1974. As the posted price rose approximately four times in three months, the global economy faced an enormous impact. The oil prices can be found in Figure 1-1. The price of gasoline soared in developed countries and governments controlled the use of energy in many ways, such as limiting heating. In March of 1974, the oil embargo on the US was removed.

As the oil-producing countries' revenues soared, they started executing large-scale economic development plans. Ironically, the oil companies' profits soared as well. The oil-producing countries were not taking profits from oil companies, but both of their profits were rapidly increasing. Both the oil-producing countries' and oil companies' cartels could gain profits because the oil price increased four times than before. We may see this in Figure 1-2 and Figure 1-3. The damage went to the consumers of each country. Although the oil-producing countries took control over oil production, the oil companies had control over production technology, transportation, and sales. The two cartels had to coexist. We may even interpret this as the two cartels becoming one giant fearsome cartel. When we think about the lesson we learned from John D. Rockefeller—even without dominating production we may still control the oil industry by dominating refinery and transportation—we can see that the oil companies were still going strong. The oil companies increased the size of the pie through cooperation.

In the past when oil companies were in control of oil production, they made profits by buying cheap oil from oil-producing countries. However, as the control of oil production was handed over to the oil-producing countries, the oil companies had to raise the oil price to make profits. No matter the intentions, if the oil price goes up, both of the cartels make profit. The fact that their interest was aligned is undeniable.

Because the oil price surged four times the original price, oil development and production increased even in areas where productions costs were high, such as the North Sea and Alaska. In addition, there were movements to increase reliance on coal and nuclear energy as well as an increase in interest of solar and wind energy.

The Second Oil Shock

As the first oil shock occurred with the Fourth Arab-Israeli War, the second oil shock occurred with the Iranian Revolution in 1978. This revolution was to overthrow Mohammad Reza Shah of the Pahlavi dynasty that was led by Ayatollah Ruhollah Khomeini. Although Ayatollah Khomeini was expelled after being arrested for criticizing the Pahlavi dynasty, he vigorously continued an anti-government struggle. In 1978, the anti-government protests expanded nationwide, and at Tehran on September 8, a large-scale bloody suppression occurred. This event became known as Black Friday. The situation rapidly deteriorated afterwards. At the end of 1978, mass protests occurred across the country and oil workers went on a strike. Oil production plummeted and exports were halted. As Saudi Arabia decreased production in January of 1979, the oil prices soared. Iran's oil exports resumed only by March of 1979, but output was unstable. In January of 1979, Mohammad Reza Shah left Iran and never returned. The Pahlavi dynasty collapsed and Ayatollah Khomeini came back to Iran, was met by an enthusiastic welcoming crowd. Through the Iranian revolution, Ayatollah Khomeini made the Islam doctrine the basis for political and social order. Islamic fundamentalism began to rapidly spread. This also affected the war in Afghanistan and the Iran-Iraq War.

Russia established a communist regime in Afghanistan and attacked Afghanistan on December 27, 1979 to prevent the spread of Islamic fundamentalism. Supported by the US, the Islamic militia Mujahidin resisted tenaciously until Russia withdrew forces in February of 1989. The exhaustive war was much like the Vietnam War. Russia faced both political and economic pressure, and this became one of the causes that made Russia collapse.

After the collapse of the Pahlavi dynasty, which was a pro-American dynasty in the Middle East, and the Russian invasion of Afghanistan, the US was concerned with their interests in the Middle East. On January of 1980, the US president Jimmy Carter announced the Carter Doctrine, which stated that the US would consider military intervention if there are any external attempts to control Middle East oil. In fact, the US supported Saudi Arabia, Israel, Egypt, Afghanistan, and Pakistan militarily. US's intervention in the Middle East still continues as of 2012.

Due to high oil prices, oil was developed all over the world in the 1980s. Although the proportion of OPEC's oil supply decreased, worldwide oil reserve market share was still absolute. According to the 2009 database of EIA (US Energy Information Administration) as seen in Figure 1-4, the share of worldwide oil reserves in 2009 were OPEC 70.1 percent, Saudi Arabia 19.9 percent, Iran 10.1 percent, Iraq 8.6 percent, Kuwait 7.8 percent, United Arab Emirates 7.3 percent, and Venezuela 7.4 percent.

On September of 1980, Iraq attacked Iran and started the Iran-Iraq War. The war lasted until August of 1988. Although Iran gave Iraq a reason to attack by breaking the border agreement, it was Ayatollah Khomeini's ideology that really threatened Saddam Hussein's regime. Complex ethnic and religious conflicts led to Iraq's preemptive strike. Oil production from both countries rapidly decreased and the oil prices rose. Eventually, oil spot prices during the second oil shock exceeded forty dollars, and the global economy fell into a crisis.

Conclusions

We may applaud to the victory of the oil-producing countries, which made an economic leap through the first and second oil shock after having their oil resources exploited for many years. However, it was the oil majors' adaptability to the new era that shined even more. The oil majors handed over the control on oil production to the oil-producing countries, but they still kept control over oil production technology, transportation, and sales. Thus, the oil majors changed their strategy from trying to gain cheap oil to safely gaining expensive oil and selling it at a higher price.

The oil-producing countries made an economic leap forward, thanks to the oil price soaring. But the oil majors also made an economic leap by achieving unprecedented performance. The interest of the oil-producing countries' cartel (dominance over oil production) and the oil companies' cartel (dominance over oil transportation and sales) was aligned. It felt as if the rise in oil prices made the pie larger for the oil market. Meanwhile, the two cartels became one fearsome cartel.

Figure 1-1. Oil Prices (WTI) (1961-1981)

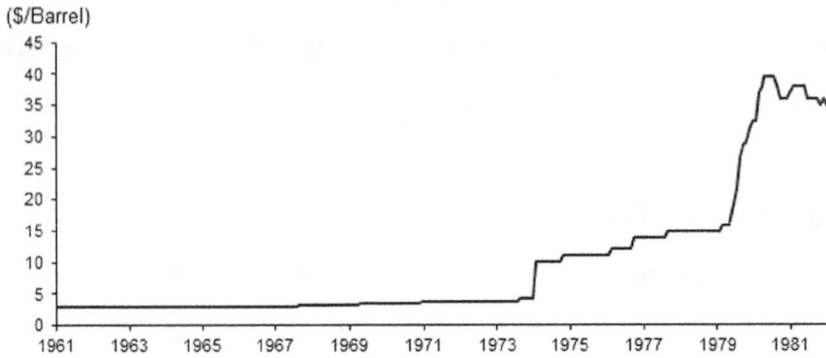

Source: BP

Figure 1-2. Saudi Arabia's Balance of Trade (1961-1981)

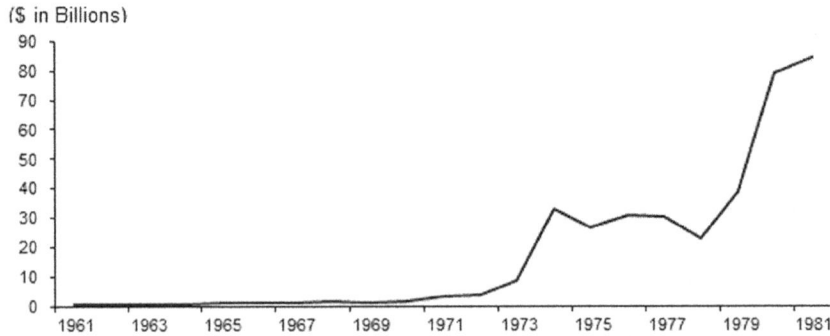

Source: IMF

Figure 1-3. Exxon's Revenue & Profit (1961-1981)

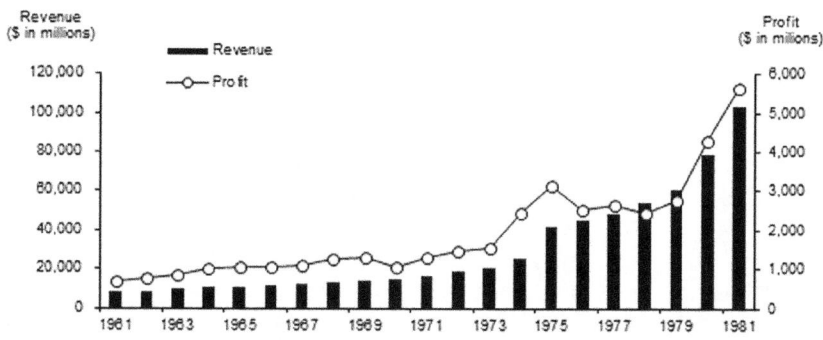

Source: SEC (US Securities and Exchange Commissions)

Figure 1-4. OPEC Countries' Market Share of Oil Reserves (1980-2009)

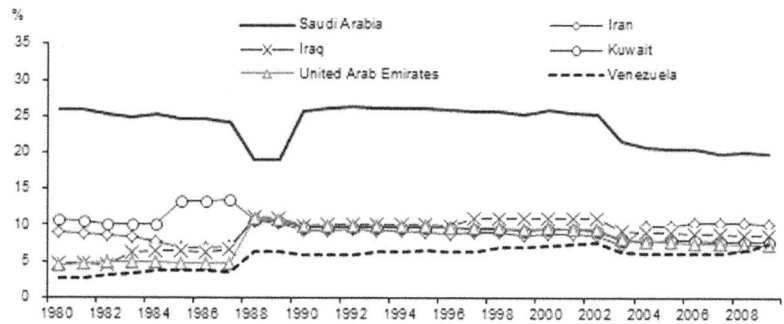

Source: EIA/BP

Part 2

History Explained with Oil and Dollars
The Oil Shock and its Effect Explained with the Oil-Dollar Composite Index

Why do we need the Oil-Dollar Composite Index?

Preview

To fully understand the oil shock and its effect, we must not only see the fluctuation of oil prices, but also the fluctuation of US dollars.

$$Oil\ Shock = \Delta Oil\ Price \times \Delta\$$$

Summary

We understand the oil shock as an economic crisis that occurred because of sudden fluctuations in the oil price. That is, "$Oil\ Shock = \Delta Oil\ Price$" ($\Delta$ is the symbol for change). This is insufficient to understand the past and pinpoint the effects. In order to completely understand the oil shock, we must first understand the leveraging role the dollar plays on oil. Therefore, we need the Oil-Dollar

Composite Index (hereafter referred as ODCI). Through an accurate understanding of the past with the ODCI, we may gain insight into the future.

$ODCI = Oil\ Price\$ \times Dollar\ Index$. By looking at the past with the ODCI, which represents the fluctuations of both the oil price and the dollar, we may clearly know who the winners and losers are. We may also see economic history in a new light.

Oil Prices are Insufficient to Explain the Oil Shock

What does it mean to say that the oil prices are insufficient to explain the oil shock? The key is in US dollars. After US President Richard Nixon closed the gold window (US dollar convertible to gold) in 1971, known as the Nixon Shock, in 1973, the monetary system of the major developed countries was changed from a fixed exchange rate system to a floating exchange rate system. And in 1976, at the IMF Interim Committee in Kingston, Jamaica, the floating exchange rate system became official.

Why is it so important that the fixed exchange rate system changed to the floating exchange rate system? In a fixed exchange rate system, one ounce of gold was fixed at thirty-five dollars. Although there were some fluctuations, the value of the dollar was fixed. The dollar acted as a unit of money for oil. As one meter is one hundred centimeters for length, one dollar was 1/35 ounces of gold. If the oil price was two dollars, then it was worth 2/35 ounces of gold.

How much would oil costing two dollars be worth in a floating exchange rate system? We couldn't know. If the oil price went up from two to three dollars, does this mean that the value also went up? We still can't know. Why? The value of the dollar changes, and we do not know the value of the dollar. Therefore, we can't know how much two dollars is worth, and we can't know if the value went up when the oil price went up from two to three dollars. Thus, we must see two dollars as two $\times \$$ and focus on the value of the dollar itself and its effects.

Let's look at simple math. Let's say that the value of oil is A, and the value of the dollar is B. In the equation $A =_2 \times B$, to know A, we must know B. We can't find out A with only the number 2. In other words, we need to know the value of the dollar. Furthermore, let's say that the equation changed from $A =_2 \times B$ to $A =_3 \times B$. Does the value of A go up? We can't know. Because the value of the dollar changes, we can't know whether B is larger or smaller than B'.

Therefore, in a floating exchange rate system, it is impossible to know the real meaning of fluctuations in oil price without knowing the value of the dollar. Thus, we need the ODCI, which considers both the dollar and the oil price. Now let's see how oil and the dollar influenced our history of economy with the ODCI.

The Dollar can be Interpreted as an Indicator of the Leverage to Oil Price

As we have seen above, a dollar in the floating exchange rate system is not just a unit of money to buy oil. The value of the dollar itself changes, and historically it was quite volatile. There were times when the value of the dollar changed dramatically. Even though the dollar had a large leveraging effect on oil prices, which would have affected the oil shock, the fluctuations in the value of the dollar was relatively neglected compared to the fluctuations in oil price. Especially when the value of the dollar fluctuated closely with the rise of oil prices but with some time gap, the movement of the dollar was undervalued. Let's see, with the ODCI, how the fluctuations in the value of the dollar affected the Latin American Debt Crisis and the Plaza Accord in 1980.

But before we go into that, let's look at oil and the oil shock using ROA (Return on Assets) and ROE (Return on Equity) as an analogy. When we analyze a company, we break down ROE into ROA and leverage. Like this, to better understand the oil shock, we need to break it down into changes in oil prices and changes in the value of the dollar.

$$\frac{Return}{Equity} = \frac{Return}{Asset} \times \frac{Asset}{Equity}$$

$$ROE = ROA \times Leverage$$

We can understand as the following:

ROE=Oil Shock, ROA=Change in Oil Price, Leverage=Change in value of the dollar

$$Oil\ Shock = \Delta Oil\ Price \times \Delta\$$$

On the other hand, we can't fully comprehend a company by analyzing only with the ROE. Full understanding occurs with the ROE considering the ROA and its leverage. Like this, the influence of the oil shock can be fully understood by seeing the change in dollar value, which acts as a leverage, and the change in oil price.

In other words, we must not underestimate the leverage and understand as if ROA and ROE are the same. This means that we must not determine the influence of the oil shock by just looking at the movement of oil price. Furthermore, sometimes the change in leverage($\Delta\$$) can be more destructive because it may also involve changes in interest rates.

Oil-Dollar Composite Index (ODCI)

First, let's check the oil price in Figure 2-1. Do you think it a coincidence that the fluctuations in the oil price suddenly became larger in 1973 when the system was changed to the floating exchange rate system?

- From 1946 to 1972, before the oil shock, fluctuations in the oil price were quite narrow (one to three dollars) and relatively stable.
- In 1973, the first oil shock rapidly increased the oil price to twelve dollars.
- In 1979, the second oil shock rapidly increased the oil price to forty dollars.

- In the 1970s, oil development and production in non-OPEC areas, such as Alaska, the North Sea, Mexico, and Russia, rapidly increased as the oil price soared. OPEC's portion of oil production decreased until 1985. It then slowly recovered afterward (Figure 2-2). In the 1980s, the Soviet Union produced twelve million barrels a day and became the number-one oil-producing country. However, after the Soviet Union collapsed in 1991, oil production plummeted until 1996. Afterward, Russia's oil production increased to the point where it made up for most non-OPEC production increases.

- From 1980 to 1988, the Iran-Iraq War broke out.

- A downward trend occurred in the oil price due to oversupply in the early 1980s.

- During the oversupply situation in 1985, Saudi Arabia increased production and had the oil price drop below ten dollars a barrel.

- In December of 1986, OPEC agreed on decreasing production to raise the oil price to eighteen dollars a barrel.

- In 1990, Iraq attacked Kuwait claiming sovereignty. The oil price soared over thirty dollars, and even reached the forty-dollar level.

- On January of 1991, led by the US, the Gulf War broke out. However, as the US government planned on releasing the SPR (Strategic Petroleum Reserve), the oil price rapidly dropped from the thirties to the twenties. The SPR is used to stabilize the oil price in case of an event that shakes the oil price. Examples would be the decrease in oil production with the damage done by Hurricane Katrina in 2005, and the civil war in Libya in 2011.

- In 1997, the oil price plummeted with the Asian Financial Crisis.

- In 1999 and 2001, Saudi Arabia decreased oil production because the oil price dropped.

- In 2003, the second Gulf War broke out. Due to political unrest, Venezuela ceased operations of national oil company PDVSA's oil production facilities. Emerging countries', such as China, oil demand increased with fast-growing economies. Due to these events, we entered the era of soaring oil prices.

- In 2004, the oil price soared as OPEC's spare capacity dropped from six million barrels (2002) to one million barrels.

- In 2005, the oil price soared when oil production decreased as Hurricane Katrina hit the Gulf of Mexico and destroyed oil production facilities.

- In 2008, WTI (West Texas Intermediate) surpassed $145 at the NYMEX (New York Mercantile Exchange). However, the oil price plummeted below the forty-dollar level with the bankruptcy of the Lehman Brothers.

- In 2011, the oil price soared as oil production decreased with political unrest in Middle East countries such as Egypt, Libya, and Bahrain.

- As of 2012, the Iran Crisis worked as an unstable factor and the oil price is moved to around the one hundred-dollar level.

Figure 2-1. Oil Prices (WTI) (1946.01-2012.01)

Source: EIA/BP

Figure 2-2. Worldwide Oil Production & Change in OPEC's Portion (1965- 2010)

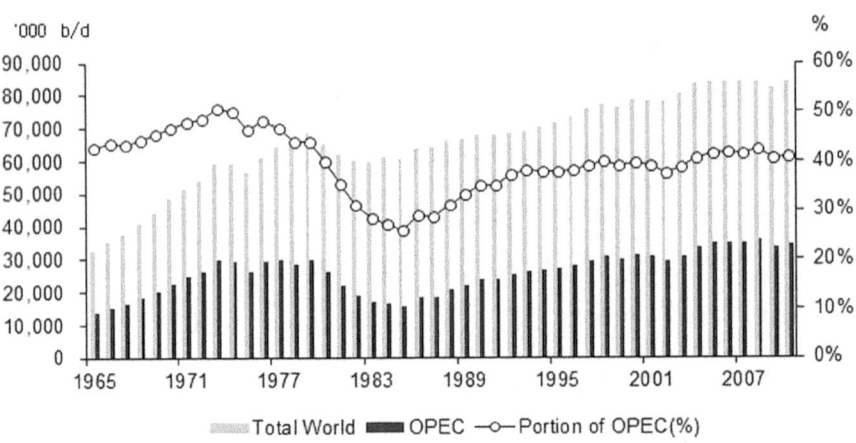

Source: BP

There are many reasons for the oil price soaring after the year 2000.

- Increase in demand of oil by emerging countries, such as China
- Rise in inflation due to low interest rates
- A weakened dollar, commodity prices remained strong
- Oil production decrease due to oil-producing countries' political unrest and natural disasters
- In 2001, George W. Bush, who had a pro-oil tendency, became the forty-third president of the US. He succeeded in being elected again and served as president until 2009.
- Due to continuous M&As by the Seven Sisters, oligopolistic control over the market increased: Chevron acquired Gulf Oil in 1985 and Texaco in 2001. Exxon and Mobil merged together in 1999. BP acquired Amoco in 1998 and Arco in 2000.

Next, let's look at the change in the value of the dollar with the dollar index (Figure 2-3).

- As World War II broke out in 1939, gold from European countries went to the US; in return, the US supplied ammunitions and grains (food). At the time, gold was the standard. So, money could be printed up to the amount of gold that the country possessed. The leakage of gold meant the decline in power. Gold reserved by the UK also rapidly decreased. The era of the British pound as the reserve currency came to an end.

- In 1944, the countries agreed on the Bretton Woods system, which is a fixed exchange rate system that has one ounce of gold worth thirty-five dollars. Since then, the US dollar became the reserve currency, and the US has maintained the position as an absolute powerhouse.

- The Marshall Plan, which was supporting Europe for four years since 1948 with twelve billion dollars, was successful, and Europe's economy was reconstructed.

- In the 1960s, the US government's spending surged as they joined the Vietnam War and executed the Great Society, a large-scale social reform program that eliminates poverty by developing education, healthcare, and so forth. Instead of increasing taxes, the US government made up a budget by issuing more dollars. US gold reserves rapidly decreased.

- In 1961, the central banks of eight countries (the US, the UK, France, and so forth) tried to stop the value of the dollar from plummeting by implementing the Gold Pool System (selling gold to stabilize the dollar), but figured out it wasn't enough and gave up in 1968.

- In 1971, the Nixon Shock, which stopped convertibility between gold and dollars, shook the roots of the gold currency standard, and the value of the dollar fell.

- In 1971, the value of the dollar dropped officially with the Smithsonian Agreement setting one ounce of gold to thirty-eight dollars (used to be thirty-five dollars).

- In 1973, the major currencies implemented the floating exchange rate system.

- In 1976, the floating exchange rate system became official at the IMF Interim Committee that was held in the capital of Jamaica, Kingston.

- In 1979, the value of the dollar surged as the dollar interest rates surged (Figure 2-4). The strong dollar lasted until 1984. During this time, many developing countries, such as Mexico, Argentina, Brazil, Venezuela, Poland, Philippines, and so forth, underwent a financial crisis.

- In 1985, the value of the dollar plunged due to the Plaza Accord.

- In 1987, the value of the dollar was stabilized with the Louvre Accord.

- In 1995, when Bill Clinton was the president, US Secretary of the Treasury Robert Rubin reduced fiscal deficits and executed a strong dollar policy. The strong dollar lasted until 2001. Once again, during this time many developing countries, such as Mexico and Argentina, underwent a financial crisis. In 1997, the Asian financial crisis occurred, and in 1998, the Russian financial crisis occurred with them declaring a moratorium.

- In the 2000s, the value of the dollar was weak because of the accumulated fiscal deficits and current account deficits. Extreme low interest rates also affected the weak dollar.

Figure 2-3. Oil Prices (WTI) & Dollar Index (1971.01-2012.01)

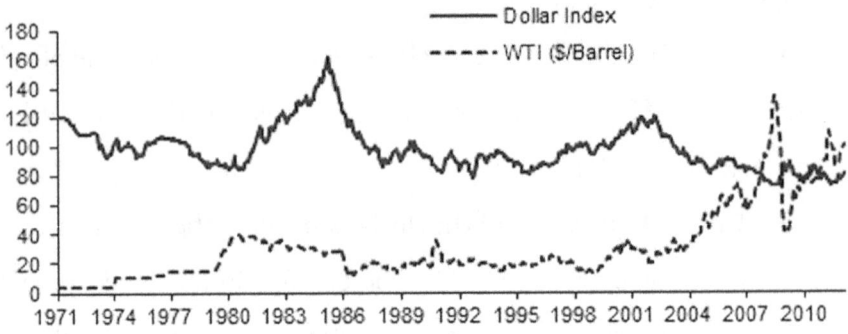

Source: FRB/BP

Figure 2-4. US Standard Interest Rate (1971.01-2012.01)

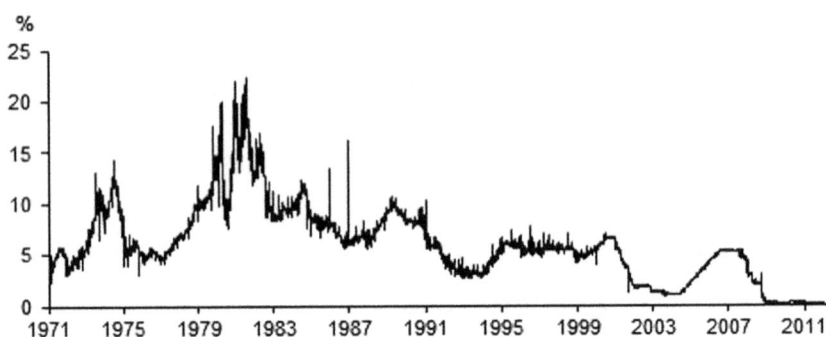

Source: FRB

Now let's finally look at the Oil-Dollar Composite Index (ODCI) (Figure 2-5). The ODCI is an index that multiplies the oil price with the dollar index. It shows the actual impact of the oil shock. *ODCI=Oil Price$×Dollar Index*. This can also be explained as the purchasing power of oil, and is the oil price that considers the change in the value of the dollar. Looking at the difference between the WTI oil prices and ODCI, we may know the difference is from the difference in the value of the dollar. We may know that the changes in ODCI are larger than the changes in the oil price because of the dollar leverage effect. The peak of the impact of the oil shock of the 1970s can be interpreted differently.

According to the oil prices, 1980 was the peak. However, according to the ODCI, the impact continuously rose until 1985. We can interpret this as the happiness index increased for countries that sold oil when the purchasing power went up. On the other hand, we may interpret the misery index increased in countries that bought oil until 1985. In other words, the ODCI becomes the happiness index or the misery index, depending on the situation they are in. For countries that imported oil, even though the oil price dropped after 1980, because the value of the dollar soared after 1979, the ODCI continuously rose, and the misery also rose until 1985. The ODCI can be seen as the happiness index and misery index for oil exporting and importing countries, respectively.

This actually greatly affects the economy. Therefore, we may see that the ODCI represents the impact of the oil shock more accurately.

ODCI actual impact of the oil shock=Oil Price $×Dollar Index

Figure 2-5. Oil-Dollar Composite Index (1971.01-2012.01)

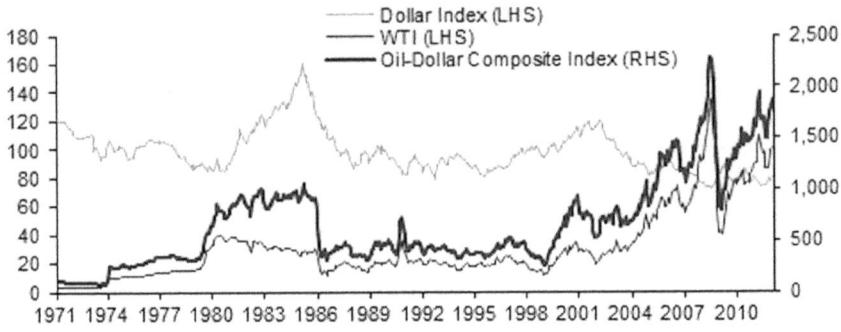

Conclusions

The dollar was only a fixed unit in the fixed exchange rate system. However, in the floating exchange rate system, the dollar is leverage to the oil price. Fluctuations increased with the floating exchange rate system, and the ODCI became meaningful. The ODCI, which considers both the fluctuations of the oil price and fluctuations of the value of the dollar, better explained the emotional changes of the oil players. The ODCI becomes the happiness index, or the misery index, depending on the country's position, and this greatly affects the economy.

The ODCI will be a new framework in understanding the oil shock of the 1970s and the economic history events of the 1980s. Through the newly perceived historical understandings, we may gain insight that foresees the future.

The Latin American Debt Crisis seen with the ODCI

Preview

In the 1980s, the economy of the developed countries became better. However, the developing countries faced a financial crisis because they were unable to manage the increasing debts.

Summary

The misery index ODCI for the developing countries, including Latin America, continuously rose, starting from the first oil shock in 1973 to 1985. This showed the collapse of the developing countries' economy and the transfer of wealth to the developed countries. To suppress the inflation due to the oil shock, the US dollar interest rate soared and the dollar became strong. Because of this, numerous developing countries were engulfed in debt problems. This tragic ending may have been prearranged since the oil shock. At least the ODCI indicator shows this as one continuous event.

The Crisis of Latin America

From the 1960s to the 1970s, developing countries borrowed dollars to develop manufacturing companies and invest in infrastructure. The burden of borrowing dollars was not that big because the value of the dollar continuously dropped. However, problems began to occur after the first oil shock in 1973. As the oil price soared, developing countries needed more dollars. The oil money of the oil-producing countries went to the developing countries through US and European banks. The increasing debt problems of the developing countries were emphasized at the fifth Non-Aligned Movement Summit held at Colombo, Sri Lanka, in August of 1976. On September 27 of 1976, the foreign affairs minister of Guyana, Frederick Wills, promoted a Third World debt moratorium at a UN meeting and shocked the world.

As the second oil shock broke out in 1979, the problem got even worse. Now the developing countries needed even more dollars. To make matters worse, since Paul Volcker became the chairman of the US Federal Reserve, interest rates continuously rose and exceeded 20 percent. At this point, developing countries needed to borrow even more dollars to pay for the interests, which increased debt. If a country was unable to gain more dollars, the country's currency was devalued and capital outflow occurred. This made the dollar even more expensive and the value of the local currency would gradually decrease. This would cause high inflation and have the country fall into a vicious cycle, eventually bringing a financial collapse.

In the 1960s and 1970s, Latin American countries, such as Brazil, Mexico, and Argentina, procured capital and achieved high-growth through industrialization. But as Mexico declared that they couldn't repay debts in August of 1982, the other Latin American countries couldn't procure dollars, even with high interest rates. The Latin American debt crisis occurred. To buy oil, dollars were needed. But as the oil price soared, more dollars were needed. So, the dollar reserves of each country ran out. Even with the oil price dropping, the burden of debt redemption for countries in debt continuously increased because the value of the dollar soared with high interest rates. We can check this with the ODCI (Figure 2-6). The interest rates soared due to high inflation, and countries with debt kept losing the ability to repay the debt, and eventually went bankrupt. In the end, the IMF issued a relief loan, but the countries were forced harsh retrenchment, and sudden devaluation of the currencies occurred. A hyperinflation, where the price level goes up a couple hundred percent, occurred, and the nation's wealth was destroyed.

According to the World Bank (Figure 2-7), foreign debt of Brazil, Argentina, and Mexico in 1970 was only $5.7 billion,

$5.8 billion, and $5.9 billion respectively. However, by 1980, foreign debt had increased to $71.5 billion, $27.1 billion, and $57.3 billion, respectively. And by 1990, foreign debt had increased to $119.3 billion, $62.2 billion, and $104.4 billion, respectively.

In 1970, Brazil, Argentina, and Mexico's external debt stocks (percent of GNI, GNI: Gross National Income) was only 13.7 percent, 19.1 percent, and 20 percent, respectively. However, Brazil became 52.7 percent in 1984, Argentina became 92.9 percent in 1989, and Mexico became 82.8 percent in 1986. Compared to gross national income, the proportion of external debt had risen immensely.

Of course, there's room for reckless management by the Latin American countries. However, there probably was no developing country that could bypass the first and second oil shock followed by a credit crunch with high interest rates. In fact, numerous developing countries experienced debt problems. The oil shock could avoid criticism when Mexico declared moratorium in 1982, because the oil price was dropping. However, ODCI, a more accurate indicator of the impact of the oil shock, continuously rose from the first oil shock in 1973 to 1985. In other words, a happiness index for developed countries, but a misery index for the developing countries, the ODCI kept rising. The debt crisis of Latin America, moreover, the debt crisis of developing countries, occurred because of the increasing ODCI. Therefore, using the ODCI, which considers both the oil price and the dollar index, helps us correctly understand the history of the economy and forecast the future.

Figure 2-6. Oil-Dollar Composite Index (1971.01-1985.03)

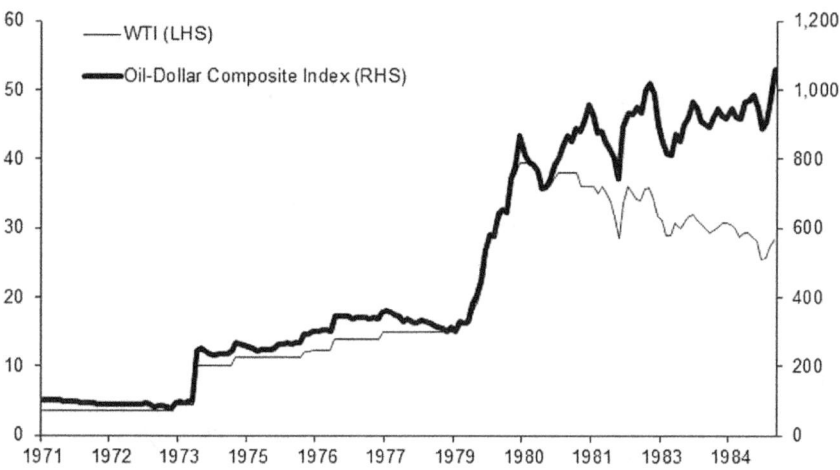

Source: FRB/BP

Figure 2-7. Brazil, Argentina, Mexico's External Debt & External Debt Stocks (percent of GNI)

	Brazil		Argentina		Mexico	
	External Debt	External Debt Stocks	External Debt	External Debt Stocks	External Debt	External Debt Stocks
Unit	USD mn	% of GNI	USD mn	% of GNI	USD mn	% of GNI
1970	5,734.5	13.7	5,809.8	19.1	6,968.6	20.0
1971	7,441.6	15.3	6,251.4	18.6	7,496.5	19.5
1972	11,518.0	19.8	6,773.1	19.8	8,209.0	18.5
1973	14,670.2	18.7	7,222.8	13.7	10,511.0	19.3
1974	22,040.0	21.1	7,628.2	10.5	13,951.6	19.7
1975	27,331.4	22.4	7,722.5	14.5	18,230.5	21.2
1976	33,341.8	22.2	9,278.4	18.1	23,966.6	27.6
1977	42,040.0	24.3	11,445.3	20.3	31,189.0	39.2
1978	54,568.2	27.8	13,276.1	23.0	35,712.3	35.9
1979	61,332.9	28.0	20,949.8	30.5	42,773.9	32.8
1980	71,526.9	31.5	27,157.0	35.6	57,377.7	30.5
1981	81,454.5	32.2	35,637.5	46.4	78,215.2	32.6
1982	93,932.3	35.2	43,614.2	55.0	86,080.6	53.3
1983	98,524.8	51.5	45,919.7	46.8	92,973.9	66.5
1984	103,861.5	52.7	48,856.8	65.1	94,829.8	57.3
1985	103,610.0	49.1	50,945.9	60.9	96,867.3	55.2
1986	109,033.7	42.6	52,449.8	49.5	100,891.4	82.8
1987	119,842.3	42.4	58,458.1	55.2	109,471.5	82.0
1988	117,409.8	37.0	58,834.1	48.7	99,215.7	56.4
1989	114,356.3	25.5	65,256.6	92.9	93,840.6	43.7
1990	119,731.6	26.6	62,232.7	46.0	104,442.0	41.1

Source: World Bank

Who is the Winner?

Let's see the results of the soaring oil price in the 1970s, followed by the soaring value of the dollar (dollar shock) in the 1980s, of the developed and developing countries with the GDP (Gross Domestic Product) growth rate and CPI (Consumer Price Index) growth rate.

We can see from Figure 2-8 to Figure 2-12 that the developed countries', such as the US, France, Germany, the UK, and Japan, CPI steadily declined until the mid-1980s, and then normalized. The GDP of these countries also grew reliably until the late 1980s.

In the case of CPI growth rate, the US was 13.5 percent in 1980, 10.3 percent in 1981, and decreased to 1.9 percent in 1986. France was 13 percent in 1980, 13.3 percent in 1981, and decreased to 2.5 percent in 1986. Germany was 5.4 percent in 1980, 6.3 percent in 1981, and decreased to -0.1 percent in 1986. The UK was 16.8 percent in 1980, 12.1 percent in 1981, and decreased to 3.6 percent in 1986. And Japan was 7.8 percent in 1980, 4.9 percent in 1981, and decreased to 0.6 percent in 1986. The great decrease in CPI growth rate brought stable price levels.

In the case of GDP growth rate, the US was -0.2 percent in 1980 but increase to 4.1 percent in 1988. France was 1.8 percent in 1980 but increased to 4.4 percent in 1988. Germany was 1.2 percent in 1980 but increased to 3.7 percent in 1988.

The UK was -2 percent in 1980 but increased to 5 percent in 1988. And Japan was 3.1 percent in 1980 but increased to 7.1 percent in 1988.

However, the CPI growth rate of developing countries Brazil, Argentina, and Mexico steadily increased until the mid-1980s, and then the prices soared in the late 1980s and brought about a hyperinflation. Under the situation of their currency exchange rate collapsing and soaring inflation, the developing countries faced continuous negative growth in GDP.

In the case of CPI growth rate, Mexico was 26.4 percent in 1980, increased to 101.8 percent in 1983, slowed down temporarily, and then rose to 131.9 percent in 1987 and 113.6 percent in 1988. In the case of Mexico, commodity prices increasing two times the original price in one year occurred quite often. We can assume the economic hardship they faced. However, compared to Brazil and Argentina's hyperinflation numbers, this was good. Brazil's CPI growth rate was already 90.2 percent in 1980, 629.1 percent in 1988, and increased to 2947.7 percent in 1990. From 1992 to 1994, it grew from 1022.4 percent to 1927.3 percent, and 2075.8 percent each year. A CPI growth rate that increases the price level ten times in one year means that the value of the currency is plummeted into becoming a mere scrap of paper. Argentina's case was similar to Brazil. The CPI growth rate was already 100.7 percent in 1980, 626.7 percent in 1984, 3079.4 percent in 1989, and 2313.9 percent in 1990. Argentina also faced hyperinflation.

We may assume that the GDP growth rate was also not so good with the currencies turning into mere scraps of paper. Mexico's GDP growth rate was quite steady as it was 9.4 percent in 1980 and 8.5 percent in 1981. However, the GDP growth rate started deteriorating in 1982.It hit -0.5 percent in 1982, -3.4 percent in 1983, and -3 percent in 1986. We could see a contrast with the developed countries' GDP growth rate rising in the late 1980s. Brazil's GDP growth rate was strong in 1980, as it was 9.1 percent. However, it started deteriorating in 1981. The GDP growth rate of Brazil was -4.4 percent in 1981, -3.4 percent in 1983, and -4.1 percent in 1990. Argentina also faced financial difficulties with the GDP growth rate being 0.7 percent in 1980, -5.7 percent in 1981, -3.1 percent in 1982, -6.9 percent in 1985, -1.9 percent in 1988, -7 percent in 1989, and -1.3 percent in 1990.

Figure 2-8. US GDP Growth Rate & CPI Growth Rate
(1980-2009)

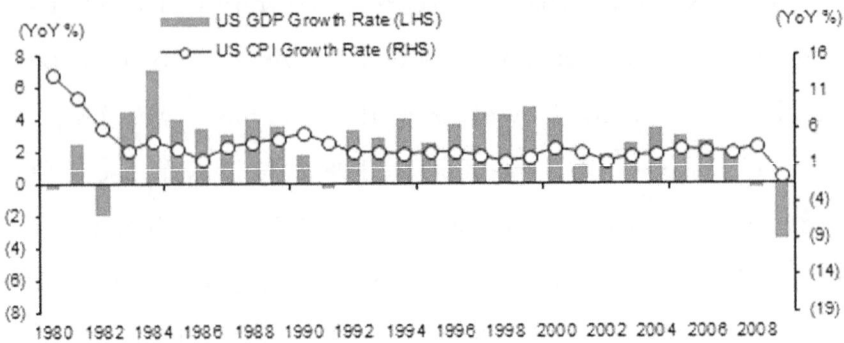

Source: UN/OECD

Figure 2-9. France GDP Growth Rate & CPI Growth Rate
(1980-2009)

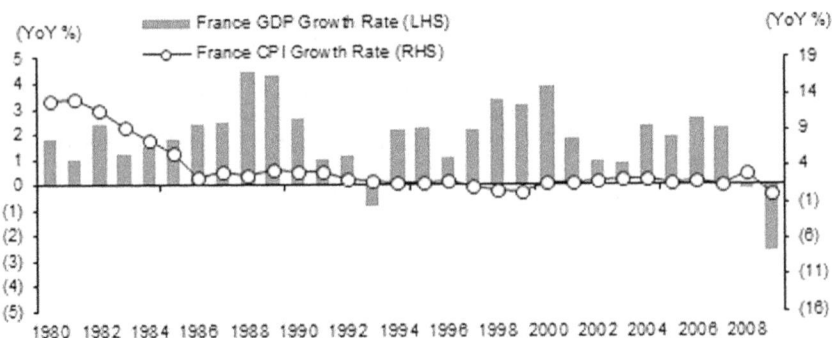

Source: UN/OECD

Figure 2-10. Germany GDP Growth Rate & CPI Growth Rate (1980-2009)

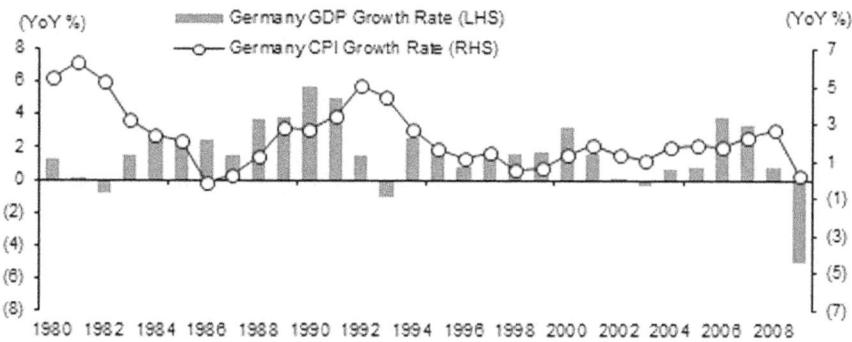

Source: UN/OECD

Figure 2-11. UK GDP Growth Rate & CPI Growth Rate (1980-2009)

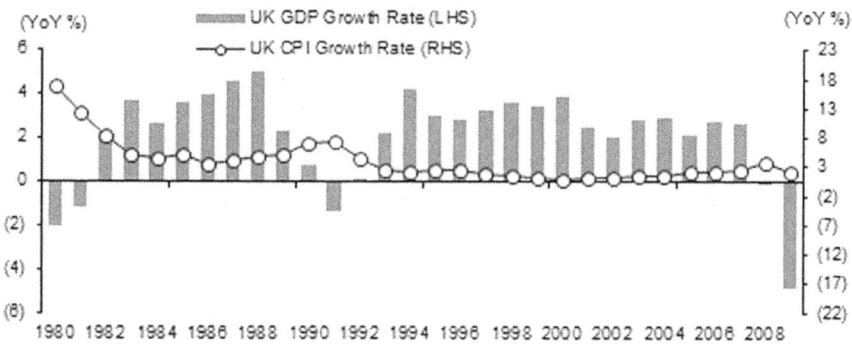

Source: UN/OECD

Figure 2-12. Japan GDP Growth Rate & CPI Growth Rate
(1980-2009)

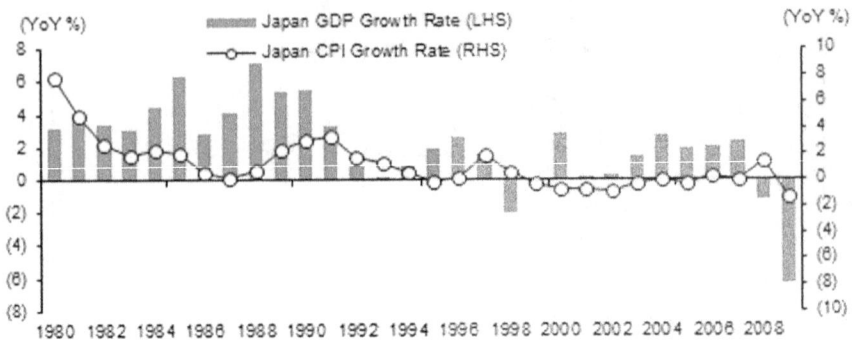

Source: UN/OECD

Figure 2-13. Brazil GDP Growth Rate & CPI Growth Rate
(1980-2009)

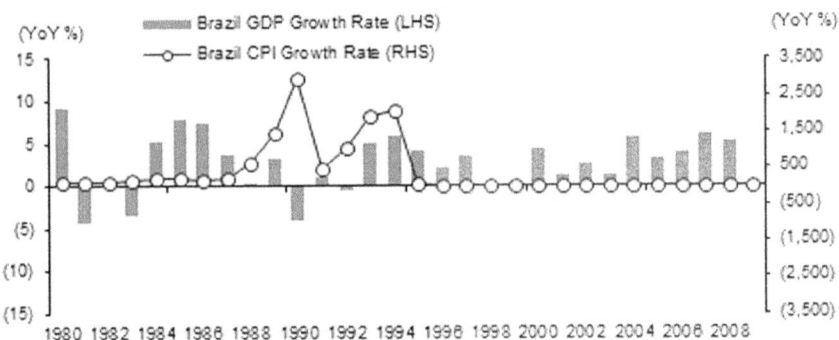

Source: UN/OECD

Figure 2-14. Argentina GDP Growth Rate & CPI Growth
Rate (1980-2009)

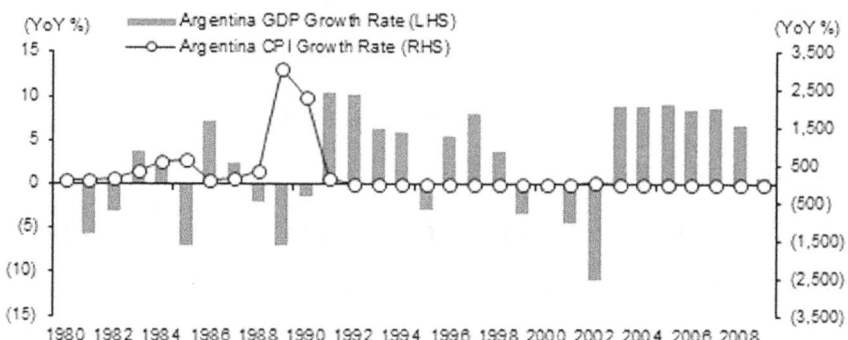

Source: UN/OECD

Figure 2-15. Mexico GDP Growth Rate & CPI Growth Rate
(1980-2009)

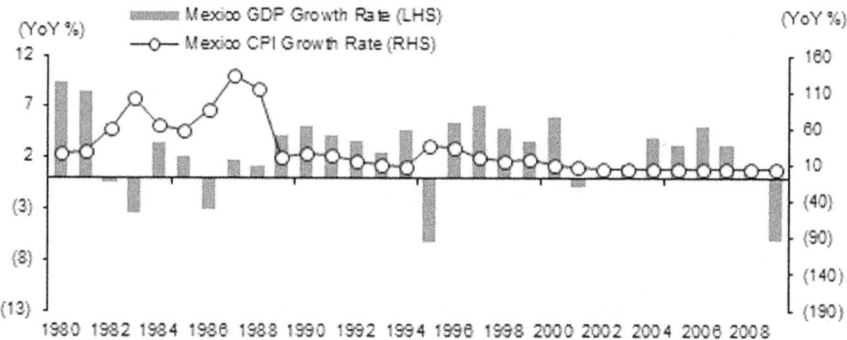

Source: UN/OECD

The developing countries' strong economy in the 1980s
also showed in the stock index. We may see this with the best-
known US index of stocks, the Dow Jones Industrial Average
(Figure 2-16). On January 2, 1970, the Dow index was 809P,

and twelve years later on January 1, 1982, it was only 875P. Afterward, the Dow index started soaring. By looking at the Dow index each year for January 1, we got 1,046P in 1983, 1,258P in 1984, 1,546P in 1986, 1,896 in 1987, 1,938P in 1988, 2,168P in 1989, 2,753P in 1990, and settled around 10,000P in 1999.

We have already seen that ExxonMobil achieved unprecedented sales and profits due to the oil price soaring with the first and second oil shock. Now let's check the stock price of the oil majors during the second oil shock (Figure 2-17). All oil majors' stock prices rose with the rise of the oil price. Chevron's stock price rose approximately three times.

The rise of the ODCI in the mid-1980s acted as a misery index for developing countries, which had them face a financial crisis, and a happiness index for oil-producing countries and oil majors. We can see the economy of developed countries quickly recover with the fall of the developing countries in the early 1980s by looking at the CPI and GDP. The oil shock followed by the dollar shock resulted in the transfer of wealth from developing countries to developed countries. This is considered to contain an important message.

Figure 2-16. US Dow Jones Index (1970-1999)

Source: FRED

Figure 2-17. Oil Price &Relative Index of Oil Majors' Stock Price (During the Second Oil Shock)

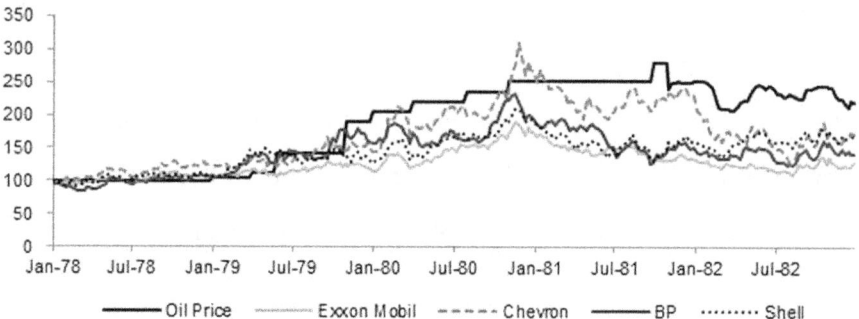

Source: Company Websites

Conclusions

The developing countries withstood quite well during the 1970s, even with the oil price soaring. However, as the value of the dollar soared with soaring interest rates, the developing countries collapsed in the early 1980s. As the oil price showed a downward trend after 1980, for developed countries, the price index stabilized, and the GDP growth rate steadily rose. On the other hand, until the mid-1980s, the ODCI, which also reflected the value of the dollar, continuously increased, and the developing countries' economies collapsed.

If the oil price surges again, developing countries not only have to worry about the increasing oil price, but also the dollar shock that may come after it. The oil price and the value of the dollar don't move separately. So, we must consider the ODCI important. The misery index shown with the ODCI can be more dreadful than the oil price graph. It also explains much more.

The Cold War and the Collapse of the Soviet Union

Preview

On the contrary to the crisis of the developing countries due to the oil price and value of the dollar soaring in the early 1980s, Russia, which was the largest oil-producing country in the 1980s, faced a crisis and collapsed in 1991 due to the oil price and the value of the dollar plummeting in 1985.

Summary

Russia (former USSR) faced political and financial difficulties because of the overheated competition of the race toward nuclear arms during the Cold War with the US, and the prolonged war in Afghanistan. The oil price, which had a major impact on Russia's income, dropped after 1980 and the economy declined. Additionally, in 1985, Saudi Arabia aggressively increased oil production and the oil price dropped below ten dollars. Russia's export income came mainly from oil, and its income rapidly decreased as the forty-dollar oil price dropped below ten dollars. In 1985, not by coincidence, the Plaza Accord event occurred, and the value of the dollar plummeted. The drop in oil price and the drop in the value of the dollar, which can be seen with the ODCI, brought a fatal financial shock to Russia. Afterward, Russia's debt soared, as did the price levels. In the late 1980s, Russia lost control over Eastern Europe, in 1989, the Berlin Wall collapsed, and in 1991, Russia collapsed.

The Cold War

Pyotr Alexeyevich Romanov (also known as Peter the Great) founded the Russian Empire in 1721. The foundation of the Romanov dynasty shook after the defeat of the Russo-Japanese War, and the Bloody Sunday, when workers demanded reforms with a peaceful demonstration but were gunned down. After World War I broke out in 1914, the economy got worse and the people suffered from extreme hardships of life. In 1917, led by industrial workers, the February Revolution ended the Russian Empire. The last emperor, Nicholas II, was abdicated and executed by a firing squad in 1918.

In 1917, Vladimir Lenin led the October Revolution (also known as the Bolshevik Revolution). The Bolsheviks took control of the regime based on Karl Heinrich Marx's ideas of communism. The White Army, composed of anti-communists, revolted, and the civil war broke out. However, the Bolsheviks ended up being victorious in 1922. The White Army was an opposing force to the Bolsheviks (Red Army), and was supported by foreign forces that opposed communism. However, this rather enhanced the legitimacy of the Red Army. The White Army lost support from its people and eventually lost the Russian Civil War.

Finally, in December 1922, the first communist country, the Soviet Union, was born. The official name was Union of Soviet Socialist Republics (USSR). As Vladimir Lenin died in 1924, Joseph Stalin ruled the Soviet Union until 1953. He successfully industrialized the country with Five-Year Plans for the National Economy of the Soviet Union. This made the Soviet Union a superpower, alongside the US.

After World War II, the US initiated the Marshall Plan, from 1947 to 1951, to reconstruct a devastated Europe and prevent the spread of Soviet Union's communism. The US gave Europe large-scale financial support, and established a military alliance with the Western countries of NATO (North Atlantic Treaty Organization). Nikita Khrushchev, who came after Joseph Stalin, ruled the Soviet Union from 1953 to 1964. To go against NATO, in 1955, he established the Warsaw Treaty Organization with the Eastern Europe communist countries. At the time, the Cold War conflict structure became clear.

During the Cuban Missile Crisis in 1962, the risk of a nuclear war heightened between the US and the Soviet Union. In 1959, the dictatorial government collapsed with the Cuban Revolution, and Cuba became a communist country led by Fidel Castro. In 1962, a US U-2 spy plane spotted construction of a Soviet Union missile base in Cuba (which was led by Nikita Khrushchev). The US President John F. Kennedy strongly opposed the base and was willing to go to war. The world had to tremble in fear of a nuclear war. Nikita Khrushchev made an agreement with the US to avoid a full-scale war. Because of this, Nikita Khrushchev's position in the Soviet Union became weak, and was also criticized by China. Eventually in 1964, he was overthrown.

Although the US was the first to create the atomic bomb in 1945, the Soviet Union followed quickly and was successful in creating an atomic bomb in 1949. In the case of the hydrogen bomb, the US succeeded in 1952, and the Soviet Union in 1953. Nikita Khrushchev stressed the importance of nuclear weapons and missiles. In 1957, the Soviet Union was the first to succeed in launching the intercontinental ballistic missile (ICBM). In October 1957, they also were the first to succeed in launching the artificial Earth satellite, Sputnik 1. This made the US nervous. In November 1957, the Soviet Union put a dog named Laika on Sputnik 2, and then became the first country to send a life form into space. This provoked the US. So, in January

1958, the US put satellite Explorer 1 on rocket Juno 1, and launched it into space. They also established NASA (National Aeronautics and Space Administration). However, the Soviet Union still dominated the field of space science. In April of 1961, Yuri Gagarin got on Vostok 1 and became the first man to fly in space. Furthermore, in March 1965, Aleksey Leonov became the first man to spacewalk, and in 1966, the Soviet Union's unmanned probe Luna 9 succeeded in landing on the moon. The US responded in 1969 by launching Apollo 11. Neil Armstrong, who was on Apollo 11, became the first man to set foot on the moon. In 1971, the Soviet Union launched the first space station Salyut into space. The US responded in 1973 by launching space station Skylab into space. In 1986, the Soviet Union sent another space station Mir into space. The US then concentrated on developing space shuttles. Starting with Columbia in 1981, the US developed Challenger, Discovery, Atlantis, and Endeavour.

In the end, the arms race between the US and the Soviet Union expanded not only to proxy wars in several countries, but also to competition in nuclear arms and space science. This incurred huge costs and served as a huge financial burden to both countries. But in the 1970s, compared to Western countries, communist countries were already clearly falling behind on economic growth. Particularly, the lack of food and necessities became acute. In the 1980s, even the Soviet Union began to have financial problems, and was unable to compete with the US on equal terms.

There was also movement in Eastern Europe to resist the Soviet Union, but this was stopped by the Soviet military. In 1953, an anti-communist resistance movement occurred in East Berlin of East Germany, but it was suppressed by Soviet troops. In 1956, the Hungarian Revolution occurred. As Hungary tried to withdraw from the Warsaw Pact, a Soviet force invaded Hungary, and many casualties occurred. In 1968, a pro-democracy movement, Prague Spring, occurred in Czechoslovakia, but was also suppressed by the Soviet army. Leonid Brezhnev, who picked up power after Nikita Khrushchev and ruled the Soviet Union from 1964 to 1982, presented the Brezhnev Doctrine one month after the invasion of Czechoslovakia. This doctrine stated that when a communist country is in danger of becoming a capitalist country, that country's sovereignty could be violated. This was a justification for the Soviet Union's military actions in the past. During the Brezhnev era, the Soviet Union continued making nuclear weapons and the amount of nuclear weapons surpassed the US after the mid-1970s. Until the Soviet Union collapsed in 1991, the Soviet Union possessed more nuclear weapons than the US.

Although the US and the Soviet Union never confronted each other directly, their proxy wars lasted a long time. The Chinese Civil War, a fight between Kuomintang (Nationalist

Government of the Republic of China) and the Communist Party of China, ended in 1949 with the communist party, led by Mao Zedong, winning. The Chiang Kai-Shek's Kuomintang, who was supported by the US, retreated to Taiwan. As China became a communist country, US President Harry S. Truman quickly increased the military budget. Afterward, the proxy wars continued with the Korean War in 1950, followed by the Vietnam War and the Afghanistan War. In addition, there were numerous proxy wars between the US and the Soviet Union in third-world countries during the 1950s and 1960s.

In the 1970s, the time of *détente* came where the tension of the Cold War was relieved. *Détente* means relief or rest in French. In 1972, US President Richard Nixon visited Moscow and signed the SALT (Strategic Arms Limitation Talks) Agreement with the Soviet Union at the US-Soviet summit. In 1973, the US army withdrew from Vietnam. However, the time of *détente* ended in 1979 when the Soviet Union invaded Afghanistan, and the tension of the Cold War heightened once again.

In 1985, Mikhail Gorbachev became the leader of the Soviet Union and introduced *perestroika* and *glasnost* policies. *Perestroika* was about restructuring and *glasnost* was about openness. Winds of change took place in the Soviet Union. He knew about the problems that the Soviet Union had and was used to the system of the Western countries by working as an ambassador in West Germany and Canada. So, he wanted to take in the advantages of capitalism. However, the economy was already stagnant, so nothing got better. Instead, suppressed problems such as nationalism and political corruption stood out.

In 1989, due to Revolutions of Eastern Europe, communist regimes were overthrown, and countries, such as Hungary, Poland, Czechoslovakia, and Romania collapsed. In 1989, the Soviet Union withdrew from Afghanistan, and in November of the same year, the Berlin Wall came down, with Germany being united in 1990. Finally, in December 1989, Mikhail Gorbachev and George Herbert Walker Bush declared the end of the Cold War at the Malta Summit. In August of 1991, a conservative communist party that was discontent with Mikhail Gorbachev's reform policies began a coup but was stopped in three days by Boris Nikolayevich Yeltsin's opposition. On December 25, 1991, Mikhail Gorbachev resigned and the Soviet Union collapsed. Boris Nikolayevich Yeltsin established the Russian Federation and became the first president.

Soviet Union's Collapse seen with the ODCI

After World War II, the Soviet Union was successful in continuously competing with the US. In the 1940s, the nuclear arms race started. In the 1950s, the Warsaw Pact was created to go against NATO and competition in missiles and space science came into full swing. Many proxy wars that lasted over a long period of time ended with the communist party victorious in several countries. However, in the 1970s, the Soviet Union could not follow the US economically, and the arms competition became an unmanageable burden. But then again, the Soviet Union spurred the development of nuclear arms, and by the mid-1970s, surpassed the number of nuclear bombs the US had. In 1979, the Soviet Union invaded Afghanistan. The war against Afghanistan, which was supported by the US, lasted for a long time until the Soviet Union withdrew their forces in 1989. This war became a political and financial burden.

The price of Soviet Union's major export, oil, was already dropping after 1980, and when Mikhail Gorbachev took office, the Soviet Union's economy was already in a serious situation. With the economic gap between the Soviet Union and the US increasing, the Soviet Union could no longer compete in arms. In the Afghanistan War, the Soviet Union experienced something similar to what the US experienced in the Vietnam War. It became a quagmire. In an economic crisis, the perestroika and glasnost policies may have been inevitable.

In this difficult situation, especially in 1985, the goddess of fortune turned its back on the Soviet Union. As seen in Figure 2-5, even though the oil price was dropping, in 1985, Saudi Arabia increased oil production and had the oil price plummet. In addition, the US, through the Plaza Accord with West Germany, the UK, France, and Japan, decreased the value of the dollar. In the 1980s, the Soviet Union was number one worldwide in oil production—even more than Saudi Arabia. With economic difficulties and increased costs due to the arms race with the US and the Afghanistan War, the plummeting of the oil price and the value of the dollar together was brutal (Figure 2-18). Figure 2-18 is a graph of the oil price (WTI) and the relative ODCI since January of 1978. The drop in oil price was critical, but the plummet in ODCI, which also considers the value of the dollar, was fatal; the Soviet Union could not recover. The price of gold (another major income of the Soviet Union) dropped from $850 in January 1980 to slightly over three hundred dollars in 1985 (Figure 2-19). After 1985, the Soviet Union's debt rapidly increased, inflation increased, and the value of the currency plummeted. Eventually, in 1991, the Soviet Union collapsed. This went along with the fact that in 1989 the Soviet Union lost control over Eastern Europe and the Eastern Europe Revolutions occurred, and that they withdrew from Afghanistan.

Figure 2-18. Oil Price (WTI Standard) & Oil-Dollar Composite
Index (1978.01-1989.12)

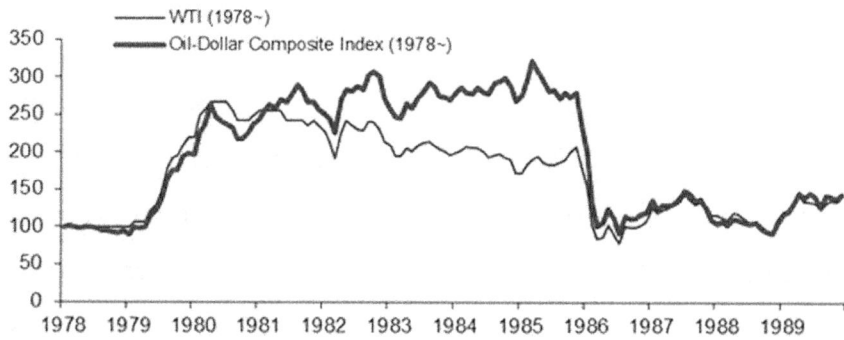

Source: EIA

Figure 2-19. Gold Price (1978.01-1989.12)

Source: World Gold Council

The Relationship between Oil and the Dollar

Usually when the dollar is weak the oil prices are strong,
and when the dollar is strong the oil prices are weak (Figure
2-5). If the investor's funds flow to the dollar by selling oil,
the oil price becomes weak and the dollar becomes strong. In

contrast, if the funds flow to oil, then the oil price becomes strong and the dollar becomes weak. Given this situation, the dollar and the oil price becoming both weak in 1985 was a very exceptional case.

According to OPEC data, the portion of oil exports out of total exports for OPEC countries was on average 77.4 percent in 2010 (Figure 2-20). Looking at each country: Algeria 66.3 percent, Angola 95.9 percent, Ecuador 55.6 percent, Iran 85.4 percent, Iraq 98.2 percent, Kuwait 93.5 percent, Libya 90.4 percent, Nigeria 87.6 percent, Qatar 40.6 percent, Saudi Arabia 83.4 percent, United Arab Emirates 37.3 percent, and Venezuela 94.7 percent. We can see that oil exports were one of the most important incomes for OPEC countries.

Oil exports on average represented 33.9 percent of GDP for OPEC countries (Figure 2-21). Looking at each country: Algeria 23.5 percent, Angola 55.4 percent, Ecuador 16.9 percent, Iran 20 percent, Iraq 40.6 percent, Kuwait 47 percent, Libya 56.4 percent, Nigeria 31.9 percent, Qatar 22.8 percent, Saudi Arabia 44.2 percent, United Arab Emirates 27.5 percent, and Venezuela 21.1 percent. We can see that oil exports were an important sector for the OPEC countries' economies.

Thus, income from oil exports was in fact an important sector of the national budget for OPEC countries. Therefore, OPEC countries were sensitive to changes in the oil price. Even if the oil price was at the level the OPEC countries wanted it to be, if the value of the dollar dropped, then from a purchasing power point of view, a budget problem occurs. For example, let's say that Saudi Arabia came up with a yearly budget calculated with the oil price as eighty dollars, and fortunately the oil price was eighty dollars. But then an event like the Plaza Accord occurred and the value of the dollar dropped. Then there becomes a problem with the planned yearly budget. Therefore, the ODCI, which considers both the oil price and the value of the dollar, is important also to the OPEC countries.

In fact, in December 1970, a resolution that allowed the posted price to be raised according to the change in exchange rate was adopted at an OPEC meeting held at Caracas, Venezuela. After the Nixon Shock that banned the exchange between the dollar and gold in August 1971, the Bretton Woods system, which set one ounce of gold to be thirty-five dollars, collapsed and the decline of the value of the dollar continued through the 1970s. In the Bretton Woods system, thirty-five dollars could always be exchanged with one ounce of gold. However, it was because of natural progression that the value of the dollar declined when the US ran out of gold and did not exchange dollars for gold. In other words, one dollar used to be 1/35 of gold, but after the Nixon Shock, the dollar became a normal currency for the country. In December 1971, leaders of each country got together and devalued the dollar by setting one ounce of gold to thirty-eight dollars at the Smithsonian Agreement to continue the Bretton Woods system. Nevertheless, the value of the dollar continuously declined and became forty-two dollars for one ounce of gold. In the end, the countries abandoned the fixed exchange rate system for the floating exchange rate system.

As the value of the dollar declined, in January 1972, OPEC increased the oil price by 8.5 percent to compensate for the loss from the depreciated dollar purchasing power. Afterward, as the value of the dollar continuously dropped, in June of 1973, OPEC increased the oil price by 12 percent. At the time, the dollar was at risk of losing its position as the reserve currency. However, as OPEC decided to take only US dollars for crude oil, the US dollar secured its status as the reserve currency. Although the dollar couldn't buy gold, it could buy oil. Oil created demand for dollars. Furthermore, the demand for dollars surged as countries needed to buy oil after the oil price surged with the two oil shocks in the 1970s. The foreign exchange reserves in each country increased. Therefore, it is important for OPEC to receive dollars for oil for the US dollar to secure its position as the reserve currency. The US can only be nothing but sensitive to OPEC changing its billing to a different currency. In 1977, OPEC considered a different billing currency for oil, but as the US greatly increased the interest rate and the value of the dollar surged, they got rid of OPEC's concerns.

As mentioned above, the OPEC countries are not only interested in the oil price, but also the value of the dollar. This is because from the viewpoint of purchasing power, the national budget is at risk. So, when the value of the dollar decreased, they raised the oil price to maintain purchasing power or they induced the value of the dollar to rise. Seeing these past behaviors, from the viewpoint of purchasing power, we can understand that the drop in both the oil price and the value of the dollar in 1985 was a tremendous blow to the OPEC countries' budgets. It was not coincidence that US-friendly Saudi Arabia's increase in oil production, which brought the decrease in oil price, and the Plaza Accord, which was an artificial event that decreased the value of the dollar, occurred at the same time. It seemed impossible for the US to hold the Plaza Accord event without the consent from OPEC, because OPEC could change the billing currency for oil. If the Plaza Accord event occurred without consultation from OPEC, the OPEC wouldn't have stayed still. According to past behavior, if the value of the dollar plummeted, OPEC would demand for the value of the dollar to rise or increase the oil price. However, OPEC did not react to the Plaza Accord in1985. On the contrary, Saudi Arabia increased production and decreased the oil price. As seen earlier, we must pay attention to the fact that the biggest victim of the plummeting oil price, and plummeting value of the dollar in 1985, was the Soviet Union.

Figure 2-20. OPEC Countries' Value of Petroleum Exports/ Total Exports (percent)

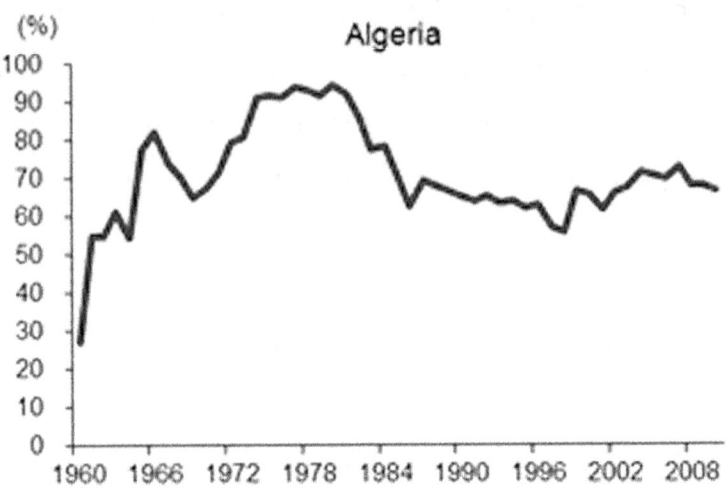

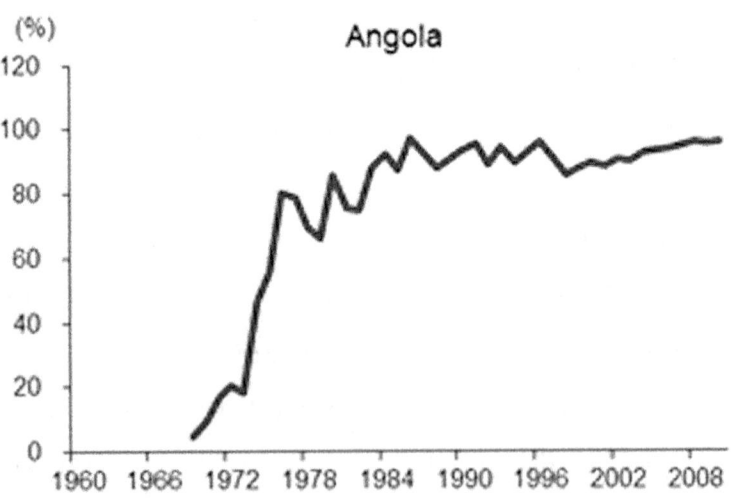

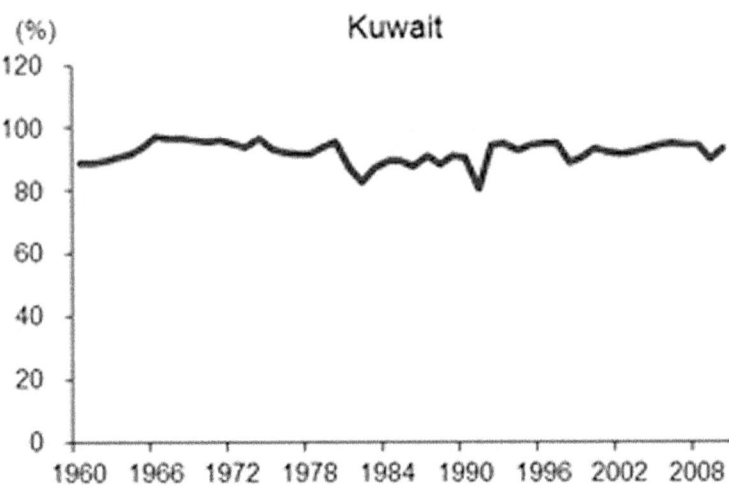

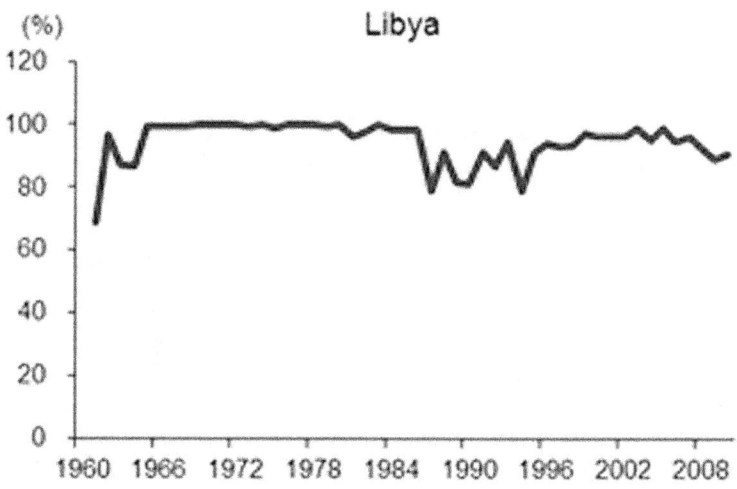

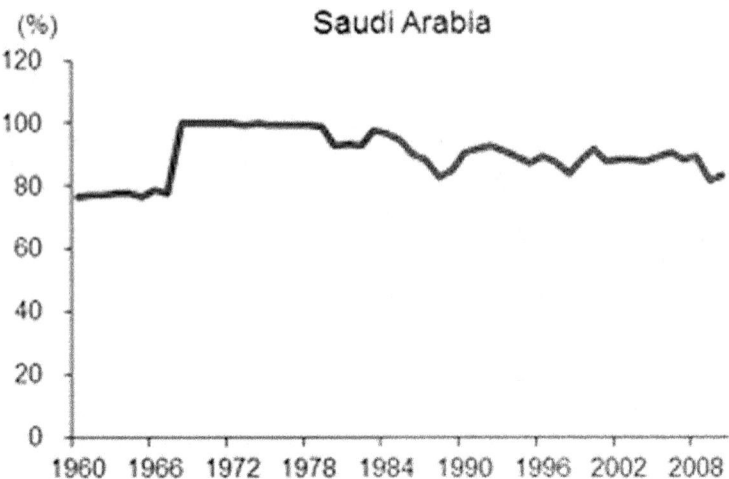

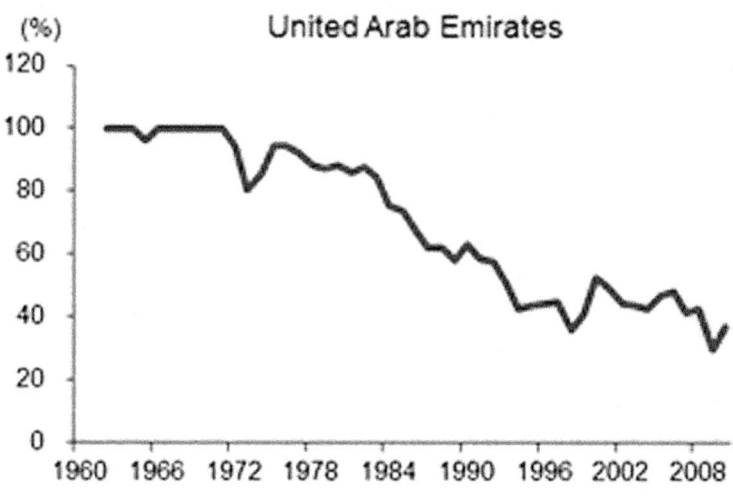

Source: OPEC

Figure 2-21. OPEC Countries' Value of Petroleum Exports/ GDP (percent)

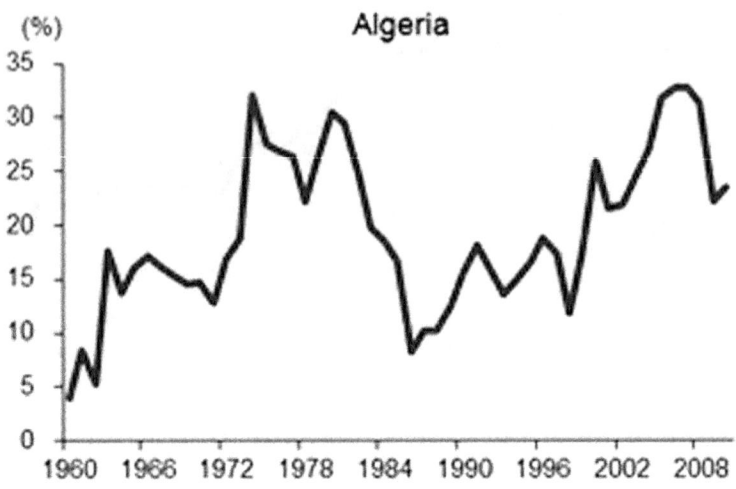

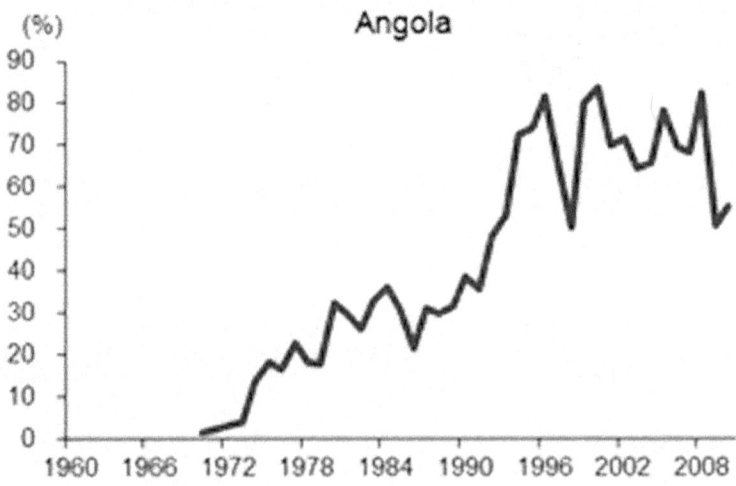

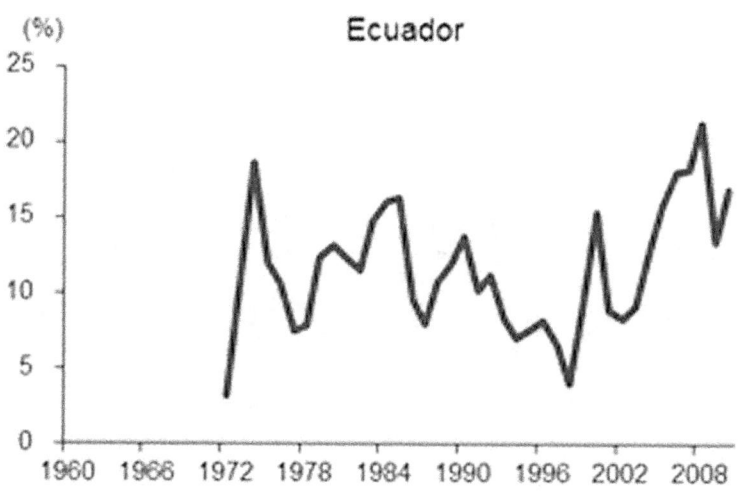

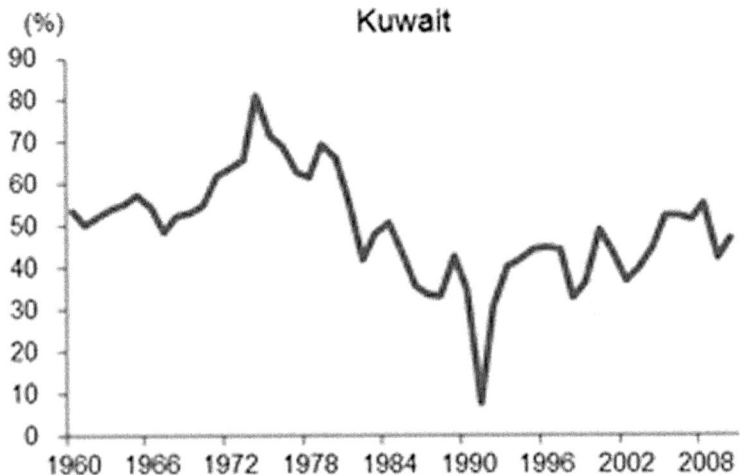

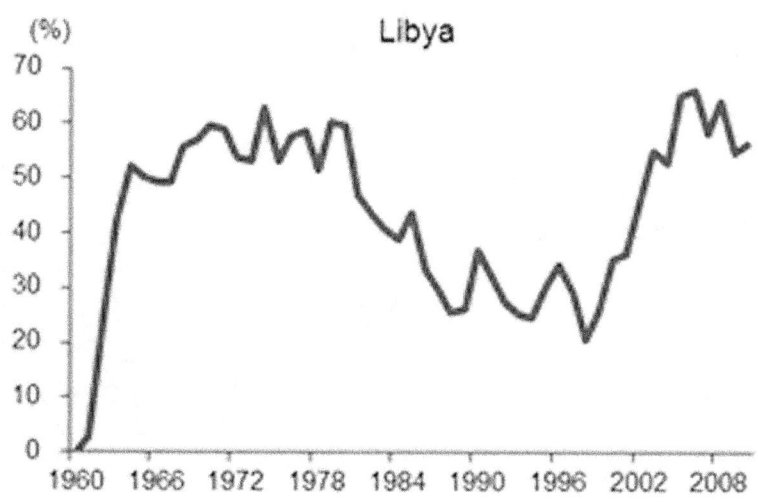

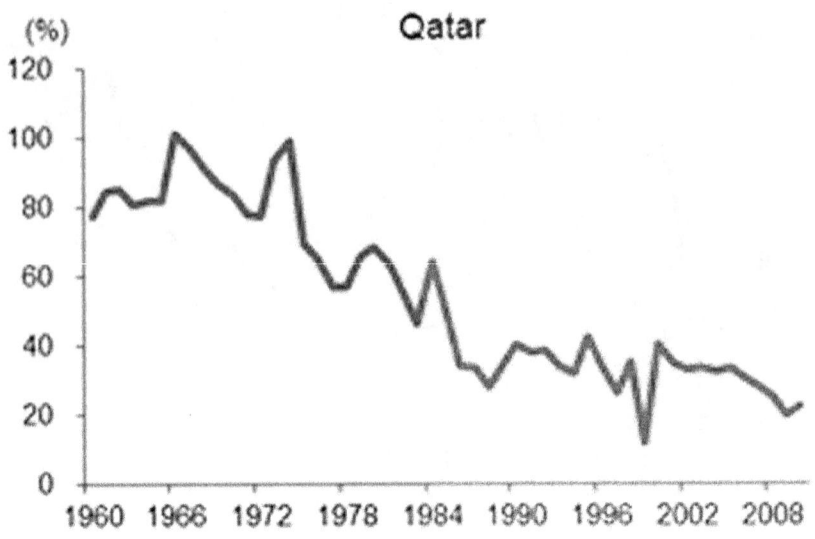

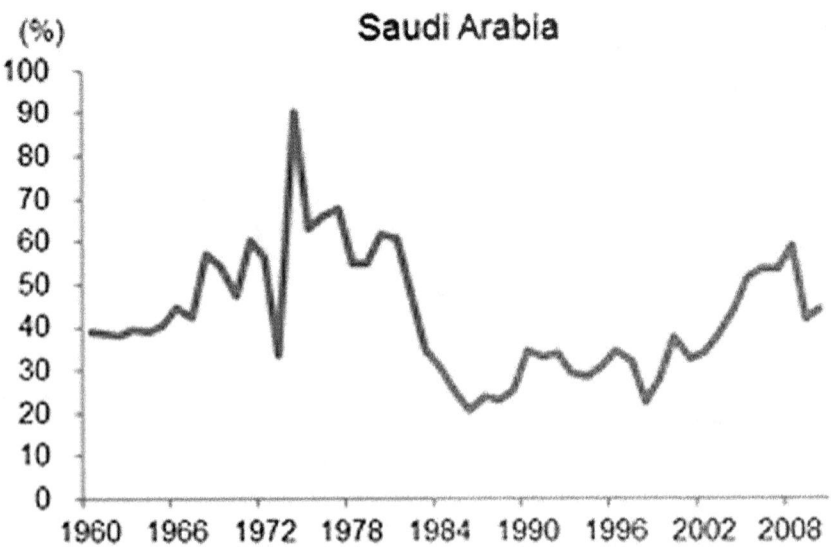

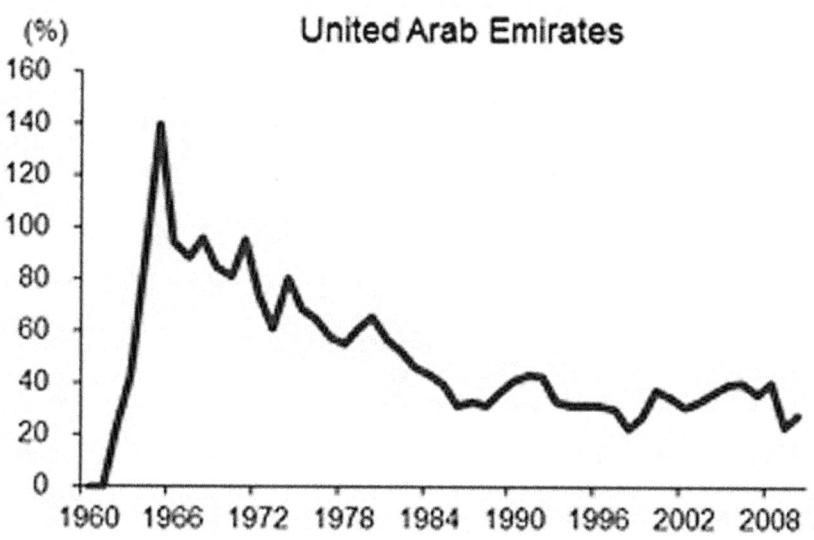

Source: OPEC

Conclusions

If the oil price and the value of the US dollar rapidly change in the same direction, we may see, with the ODCI, that the impact is great. The first and second oil shocks, followed by the surge in the value of the dollar represented by the ODCI, were happiness indexes to the developed countries and misery indexes to the developing countries. The drop in both the oil price and the value of the dollar in 1985, represented by the ODCI, became misery indexes for the 1980s' largest oil-producing country—the Soviet Union. From the viewpoint of purchasing power, the ODCI also reflects the budget of the OPEC countries.

The dollar and the oil price are closely related, and this can be seen in many historical examples. Therefore, ODCI, which considers both the oil price and the value of the dollar, is important in understanding history and gaining insight. As a result, new light is shed as the developing countries and the Soviet Union are seen as victims. We can also acknowledge the importance of the dollar in the oil shock.

$$ODCI\ (actual\ influence\ of\ the\ oil\ shock) = Oil\ Price\ \$ \times Dollar\ Index$$

Part 3

The Third Oil Shock

History Repeats Itself

Will the Third Oil Shock Come?

Preview

The oil price cannot be explained only with supply and demand. We may predict the direction of the oil price by understanding the interaction mechanism between oil and the dollar.

Summary

It is hard to explain the oil price with only supply and demand. Interests of numerous countries, circumstances of the era, and the relationship between oil and the dollar have a lot of influence on the oil price. Today's global interest is hinting toward the rise of the oil price, and this is expected to be realized soon. The transfer of wealth from 1970 to 1980 can be repeated.

Supply & Demand is Insufficient to Explain the Oil Price

Can we explain the first oil shock, when the price increased fourfold in 1973, with supply and demand? If so, when the oil embargo was lifted and the supply was normalized, why didn't the oil price go back down? Basically, power was transferred from the oil majors to the oil-producing countries and the oil price, which had been sold for an abnormally low price, was normalized. The cut in oil production and the oil embargo during the first oil shock was nothing more than the oil-producing countries showing off their power. In other words, decrease in oil production and the oil embargo during the first oil shock wasn't the cause for the oil price to rise, but only a phenomenon. The real reason was the shift in the balance of power. In September of 1970, when Occidental Petroleum accepted Libya's demand of increasing the tax rate and the posted price, the oil-producing countries already had the upper hand in negotiating with the oil companies. This led to the victory of the oil-producing countries with the Tehran agreement in February of 1971. The influence of the victory spread to nationalization of oil resources, and Iraq, Saudi Arabia, Kuwait, Nigeria, and Venezuela nationalized their oil. The primary reason for the first oil shock is usually suggested as the attack on Israel by Egypt and Syria in the Fourth Arab-Israeli War. However, this was also an expression of confidence. The

Arab countries lost the war with Israel, which was supported by the US, but gained benefits with the oil price soaring. In the second oil shock, which occurred because of the Iranian Revolution in 1978, the oil price rose from approximately ten dollars to forty dollars, and this cannot be explained only with supply and demand.

Ironically, even though a significant portion of the oil majors' power was handed over to the oil-producing countries, the oil majors achieved unprecedented profits during the first oil shock. Additionally, the profitability of North Sea oil and Alaska oil improved after having a hard time in development due to high production costs. The oil majors once again achieved unprecedented profits during the second oil shock.

Although a lot of worldwide consumers suffered from the soaring oil price during the first and second oil shock, the most obvious victim seen with the ODCI was Latin America and third-world countries. An obvious beneficiary of the oil price and gold price increase was Russia. Thanks to that, in the mid-1970s, Russia was able to outrun the US in the nuclear arms, and also gain the upper hand in space science. However, this confidence led to the invasion of Afghanistan, and became an increasing financial burden along with the plunging oil and gold prices.

What did the supply and demand of oil tell us when the oil price soared after 2003? Can we find the reason that the oil price jumped from slightly over twenty dollars in 2000 to the $140 level in 2008? Figure 3-1 shows worldwide supply and demand of oil, with supply and demand, and Figure 3-2 shows the change in supply and demand more accurately—but this is still not enough to explain the oil price increase in 2000. In 2003 and 2004, there was good demand, but because the supply also increased, there seemed to have been no problem. The weak dollar could be suggested as the reason, but it is hard to accept the fact that a weak dollar could increase the oil price not just several percent but several hundred percent. Details of this can be found in Figure 3-3 and Figure 3-4. China's demand increased 12 percent in 2003 and 16.1 percent in 2004, but because this is part of worldwide increase in demand, we can see that this was solved with increase in supply. After 2005, the increase in demand decreased each year until 2008 at 3.1 percent, 7.5 percent, 5.6 percent, and 1.3 percent respectively each year. Absolute demand of oil a day was 5.6 million barrels in 2003 and 6.5 million barrels in 2004, which is very small compared to OECD's supply of 48.7 million barrels in 2003 and 49.5 million barrels in 2004. Afterward, China's increase in demand decreased, so this can't explain the oil price soaring to $140. Developed countries had good times in the 1980s and 1990s based on stable oil prices, but when China showed high growth, they could not obtain cheap oil.

Let's take a closer look at Figure 3-3. From 1993 to 2011, total demand increased 31.6 percent from 67.7 million barrels to 89.1 million barrels and total supply increased 30.7 percent from 67.7 million barrels to 88.5 million barrels.

However, OECD countries' increase in demand was only 5.4 percent from 43.3 million barrels to 45.6 million barrels. Moreover, only North America increased 11.9 percent while Europe and the Asia-Pacific region didn't show any increase. On the other hand, non-OECD countries' demand increased 78 percent from 24.4 million barrels to 43.4 million barrels. China especially showed the highest growth rate of 217 percent.

In the case of supply, OPEC's growth rate was 36.6 percent and non-OPEC's growth rate was 27 percent. From the non-OPEC countries, Russia and Latin America was notable with a growth rate of 72 percent and 100 percent, respectively from 2003 to 2011.

China's supply increased 41.4 percent, from 2.9 million barrels in 1993 to 4.1 million barrels. But the problem was that the demand increased 217 percent, from three million barrels in 1993 to 9.5 million barrels in 2011. From a self-sufficiency standpoint, in 1993, 2.9 million barrels of supply covered almost all of the three million barrels of demand. However, in 2011, only 4.1 million barrels of supply covered a part of 9.5 million barrels of demand. The other 5.4 million barrels of oil had to be sourced from abroad. Considering that China's GDP per capita is 1/10 of the US, and that China's automobile distribution rate is 1/10 of the US, we can predict that China's oil demand will continuously increase, along with the dependence on foreign oil.

Russia, on the other hand, decreased in demand and increased in supply from 2.2 million barrels in 1993 to 8.9 million barrels in 2011. In other words, both Russia and China increased in supply, but only Russia's net supply increased because their demand decreased; whereas, China's demand surged to the point that they were no longer self-sufficient, and now they have to depend on foreign oil. For Russia, the oil price needed to rise, whereas, for China it needed to decrease. The two countries are opposed in energy. As Russia struggled when the oil price dropped in 1985, China was in the position of suffering when the oil price rose. OECD's oil consumption reached its peak in 2005 and has decreased since then, whereas, as of 2012, China's demand increases every year. China already suffers from high inflation due to excessive investment in the past. If the oil price soars, and another oil shock occurs, the biggest victim will most likely be China.

Fortunately, because China's financial market isn't completely open and they have enough dollars because their foreign exchange reserves are number one worldwide, even if an oil shock occurs, they seem to be safe from the dollar shock that could follow it. However, since their economy is gradually growing, they will have to gradually open their financial markets. In fact, they are planning to completely open their financial markets in three phases over the next ten years. Additionally, as China's growth policy has changed from investment-driven growth to consumption-oriented growth, they are planning to double the 2010 average salary by 2015. As seen in Figure 3-5, China's average income has maintained a high growth rate. Although it depends on how well China uses their policies to control the economy, it is most likely that the high growth rate in income will harm the existing export competitiveness. Already, many foreign companies have moved their factories from China to countries with more cheap production costs, such as Vietnam and Indonesia. Additionally, developed countries, especially the US, that think China has achieved a huge trade surplus by using the artificially under-valued Yuan currency as a weapon and is creating a global trade imbalance, are pressuring China to revalue the Yuan currency upward. This will also most likely harm China's export com-petitiveness and could later on lead to the reduction of foreign exchange reserves. If China's financial market gradually opens and China's foreign exchange reserves decrease, there is a high chance of another dollar shock.

After the developing countries, especially Latin America, experienced difficulties in the 1980s, they occasionally suf-fered from crises. After the Soviet Union collapsed in 1991, Russia experienced the Russian moratorium in 1998. Many

Asian countries experienced the Asian financial crisis in the 1990s. Although the US did not experience a foreign exchange crisis because the dollar is the reserve currency, superpower US experienced difficulties when the Lehman Brothers went bankrupt in 2008. Europe also experienced successive financial crises and faced difficulties. China has maintained a good balance between control and openness amidst all the financial crises going on. But as China goes along with the global economy, weaknesses will be gradually exposed. And its beginning will be oil.

Figure 3-1. Worldwide Oil Supply & Demand (1993-2011)
(Unit: MMbpd)

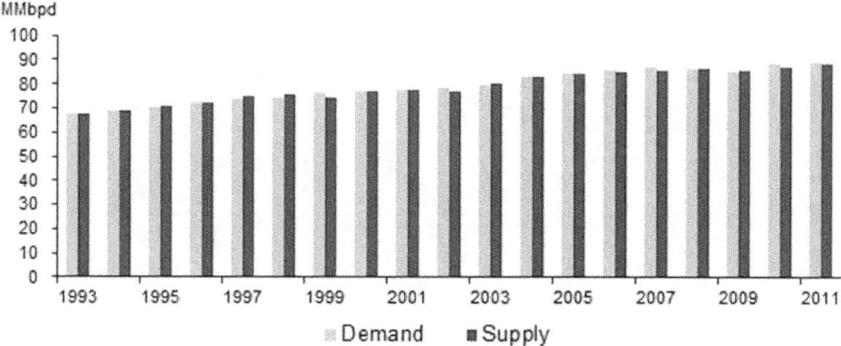

Source: IEA | MMbpd (million barrels of oil per day)

Figure 3-2. Worldwide Oil Supply & Demand Growth Rate
(1994-2011)

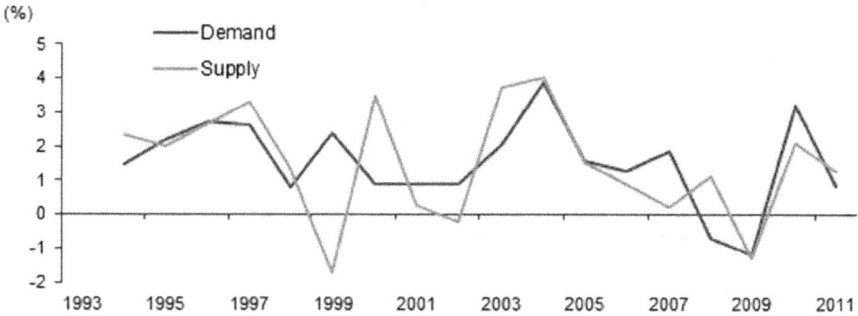

Source: IEA

Figure 3-3. Worldwide Oil Supply & Demand Data (1993-2011)

Million Barrels/Day	1993	1994	1995	1996	1997	1998	1999	2000	2001	2002	2003	2004	2005	2006	2007	2008	2009	2010	2011
Total Supply	**67.7**	**68.7**	**70.2**	**72.1**	**74.0**	**74.6**	**76.4**	**77.1**	**77.8**	**78.5**	**80.1**	**83.2**	**84.5**	**85.6**	**87.2**	**86.6**	**85.6**	**88.3**	**89.1**
OECD	43.3	44.5	44.9	46.0	46.8	47.0	48.0	48.0	48.0	48.0	48.7	49.5	49.9	49.5	49.3	47.6	45.6	46.2	45.6
North America	21.0	21.7	21.6	22.2	22.7	23.1	23.9	24.1	24.1	24.2	24.6	25.5	25.6	25.4	25.5	24.2	23.3	23.8	23.5
Europe	14.3	14.4	14.7	15.0	15.1	15.4	15.4	15.2	15.4	15.3	15.4	15.6	15.7	15.7	15.5	15.2	14.7	14.6	14.3
Asia-Pacific	8.0	8.4	8.6	8.8	8.9	8.4	8.7	8.7	8.6	8.5	8.6	8.6	8.6	8.4	8.1	8.1	7.7	7.7	7.9
Non-OECD	24.4	24.2	25.4	26.1	27.2	27.6	28.5	29.1	29.7	30.5	31.4	33.6	34.6	36.0	37.8	38.9	39.9	42.2	43.4
Russia	5.7	4.6	4.3	3.9	3.9	3.8	3.7	3.8	3.9	3.8	3.9	3.9	3.9	4.0	4.1	4.2	4.2	4.5	4.7
China	3.0	3.0	3.3	3.6	3.9	4.1	4.3	4.6	4.7	5.0	5.6	6.3	6.7	7.2	7.6	7.7	8.1	9.1	9.5
Asia (etc.)	5.4	5.5	6.2	6.5	6.9	7.0	7.5	7.7	7.8	8.1	8.3	8.5	8.9	9.1	9.7	9.7	10.1	10.4	10.7
South America	3.8	4.1	4.3	4.5	4.8	4.9	5.0	4.9	5.0	4.9	4.8	5.1	5.2	5.4	5.7	6.0	6.0	6.3	6.5
Middle East	4.1	4.3	4.4	4.5	4.6	4.8	5.0	5.1	5.3	5.4	5.5	5.9	6.3	6.5	6.9	7.3	7.5	7.8	8.0
Africa	2.0	2.1	2.2	2.2	2.3	2.3	2.5	2.4	2.5	2.6	2.7	2.8	2.9	2.9	2.9	2.9	2.9	3.4	3.4
Total Demand	**67.7**	**69.3**	**70.7**	**72.6**	**75.0**	**76.0**	**74.7**	**77.3**	**77.5**	**77.3**	**80.2**	**83.5**	**84.8**	**85.5**	**85.7**	**86.7**	**85.6**	**87.4**	**88.5**
OPEC	26.2	26.6	27.4	29.7	29.7	30.6	29.2	30.3	30.3	30.6	30.8	33.3	34.8	35.2	36.1	36.1	34.1	34.8	35.8
Saudi Arabia	8.0	7.9	7.9	7.9	8.1	8.1	7.5	8.0	7.7	7.4	8.5	8.6	9.1	8.9	8.5	8.9	7.9	8.1	N/A
Iran	3.7	3.6	3.7	3.7	3.6	3.6	3.5	3.7	3.7	3.4	3.8	3.9	3.9	3.9	4.0	3.9	3.7	3.7	N/A
Iraq	0.5	0.5	0.6	0.6	1.2	2.1	2.5	2.6	2.4	2.0	1.3	2.0	1.9	1.9	2.1	2.4	2.4	2.4	N/A
Non-OPEC	41.5	42.7	43.4	44.5	45.3	45.4	45.5	46.6	47.2	48.6	49.5	50.2	50.0	50.4	50.7	50.6	51.5	52.6	52.7
North America	14.0	14.0	14.0	14.3	14.6	14.5	13.9	14.2	14.2	14.4	14.4	14.4	13.9	13.9	13.9	13.3	13.6	14.1	14.5
Europe	5.2	6.1	6.4	6.7	6.7	6.7	6.8	6.8	6.6	6.6	6.4	6.1	5.7	5.3	5.0	4.8	4.5	4.1	3.8
Russia	7.9	7.4	7.2	7.1	7.3	7.3	7.5	8.0	8.7	9.5	10.5	11.4	11.8	12.3	12.8	12.8	13.3	13.5	13.6
China	2.9	2.9	3.0	3.1	3.2	3.2	3.2	3.3	3.3	3.3	3.4	3.5	3.6	3.7	3.7	3.7	3.9	4.1	4.1
South America	2.1	2.2	2.4	2.6	2.8	3.0	3.2	3.4	3.2	3.4	3.2	3.5	3.5	3.6	3.6	3.7	3.9	4.1	4.2
Africa	1.8	1.9	1.9	1.9	2.0	2.0	2.1	2.0	2.0	2.1	2.2	2.5	2.5	2.5	2.6	2.6	2.6	2.5	2.5
Biofuel	0.3	0.3	0.3	0.3	0.3	0.3	0.3	0.3	0.3	0.4	0.5	0.5	0.6	0.8	1.1	1.4	1.6	1.8	1.8
Processing Gains	1.4	1.4	1.5	1.6	1.6	1.7	1.8	1.8	1.8	1.8	1.9	1.9	2.0	2.0	2.0	2.0	2.0	2.1	2.2
Surplus/Deficit	0.0	-0.6	-0.5	-0.5	-1.0	-1.4	1.7	-0.2	0.3	1.2	-0.1	-0.3	-0.3	0.1	1.5	-0.1	-0.0	0.9	0.6

Source: IEA

Figure 3-4. Worldwide Oil Supply & Demand Growth Rate Data (1994-2011)

GROWTH (%)	1994	1995	1996	1997	1998	1999	2000	2001	2002	2003	2004	2005	2006	2007	2008	2009	2010	2011
Total Supply	1.5	2.2	2.7	2.6	0.8	2.4	0.9	0.9	0.9	2.0	3.9	1.6	1.3	1.9	-0.7	-1.2	3.2	0.8
OECD	2.8	0.9	-0.5	2.4	1.7	0.4	2.1	-0.0	0.1	-0.1	1.4	1.7	0.7	-0.7	-3.5	-4.1	1.1	-1.1
North America	3.3	3.5	2.8	2.0	2.3	1.8	3.5	0.9	0.0	0.3	1.7	3.5	0.5	-0.8	0.3	-5.0	-3.8	2.0	-1.1
Europe	0.7	2.1	2.0	0.0	0.7	2.0	0.0	-1.2	1.1	-0.3	0.7	0.7	0.8	0.0	-1.3	-0.5	-4.8	-0.5	-2.1
Asia-Pacific	5.0	2.4	2.3	1.1	1.1	-5.6	3.6	-0.5	-1.3	-0.7	1.8	-1.3	0.9	-1.6	-0.9	-3.5	-5.1	1.7	0.5
Non-OECD	-0.8	4.1	3.6	4.2	1.5	3.3	-2.6	2.1	2.1	2.7	3.0	7.0	3.0	4.0	5.0	2.9	2.6	5.6	3.0
Russia	-19.3	-6.5	-9.3	0.0	-2.6	4.5	2.7	0.0	0.0	2.6	0.0	2.7	7.5	2.5	2.4	-0.5	6.7	5.2
China	0.0	10.0	9.1	8.3	5.1	4.5	7.0	2.2	6.4	12.0	16.1	3.1	7.5	5.6	1.3	4.7	12.5	4.9
Asia (etc)	5.8	12.7	4.8	6.2	1.4	7.1	2.7	1.3	3.8	2.5	6.0	1.1	2.2	5.5	1.0	4.1	3.0	2.9
South America	7.9	4.9	4.7	6.7	2.1	7.1	-2.0	2.0	2.0	-2.0	6.3	2.0	3.6	5.6	5.3	-0.2	5.2	2.9
Middle East	4.9	2.3	2.3	2.2	4.3	4.2	2.0	3.9	1.9	1.9	7.3	6.8	3.2	6.2	5.8	3.2	3.9	2.4
Africa	5.0	4.8	0.0	4.5	0.0	8.7	-4.0	4.2	4.0	3.6	3.7	3.6	0.0	6.9	6.5	0.9	1.8	-1.2
Total Demand	2.4	2.0	2.7	3.3	1.3	-1.7	3.5	0.3	-0.2	3.7	4.0	1.5	0.9	0.2	1.2	-1.3	2.1	1.3
OPEC	1.5	3.0	2.6	5.7	3.0	-4.6	5.4	-1.6	-4.9	6.9	8.2	4.1	1.0	-0.5	3.2	-5.5	2.1	2.9
Saudi Arabia	-0.8	0.5	-0.4	2.1	0.1	-7.0	6.4	-3.8	-4.2	14.9	1.4	5.3	-1.4	-5.0	5.0	-11.3	3.0	N/A
Iran	-1.1	1.1	0.5	-1.9	0.8	-3.6	5.1	0.5	-8.1	11.2	4.0	-1.3	0.8	1.8	-2.0	-4.1	-1.1	N/A
Iraq	10.4	3.8	5.5	98.3	83.5	19.4	2.0	-8.2	-14.8	-34.3	50.8	-9.0	5.0	10.0	13.9	2.1	-2.9	N/A
Non-OPEC	2.9	1.6	2.5	1.8	0.2	0.2	2.3	1.5	2.8	1.9	1.4	-0.4	0.8	0.7	-0.2	1.8	2.1	0.2
North America	0.0	0.0	2.1	2.1	-0.7	-4.1	2.2	0.3	0.8	0.6	-0.6	-3.3	0.1	-0.4	-4.0	2.3	3.7	2.8
Europe	17.3	4.9	4.7	0.0	0.0	1.5	-0.1	-0.2	-0.5	-3.9	-3.6	-7.5	-6.9	-6.5	-3.6	-6.3	-0.9	-7.3
Russia	-6.3	-2.7	-1.4	2.8	0.0	2.7	6.4	8.4	9.8	10.2	9.2	3.5	4.0	4.1	-0.1	3.9	1.5	0.7
China	0.0	3.4	3.3	3.2	0.0	0.0	1.6	0.9	1.8	1.5	3.5	3.4	1.9	0.8	1.9	2.6	5.1	0.0
South America	4.8	9.1	8.3	7.7	7.1	6.7	-0.9	0.9	4.7	0.6	-1.8	5.1	3.2	-0.3	3.4	5.4	5.1	2.4
Africa	5.6	0.0	0.0	5.3	0.0	5.0	-4.8	2.0	3.9	4.2	11.8	0.4	2.4	2.8	-0.4	0.0	-3.8	0.0
Biofuel	0.0	0.0	0.0	0.0	0.0	0.0	-10.0	7.4	27.6	29.7	10.4	17.0	27.4	34.2	32.1	14.3	12.5	0.0
Processing Gains	0.0	7.1	6.7	0.0	6.3	5.9	2.2	-1.1	1.1	4.3	1.0	1.0	3.6	-0.5	-1.0	0.0	5.0	4.8

Source: IEA

127

Figure 3-5. China's Average Income (1970-2011)

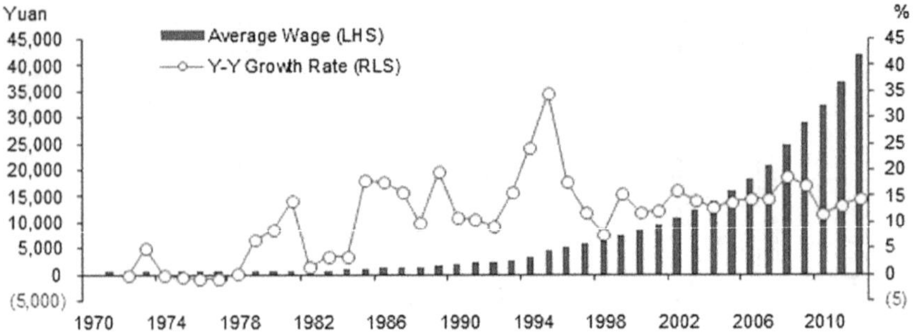

Source: National Bureau of Statistics of China

Interaction between Oil and the Dollar

To understand oil, it is important to correctly understand the reserve currency, the dollar. To understand this, it is important to know the difference between the gold currency standard of the fixed exchange rate system where gold is exchanged with a fixed amount of gold and the reserve currency system (dollar) of the floating exchange rate system that evolved after the Nixon Shock, when the dollar was no longer allowed to be traded for gold.

Before the Bretton Woods system came into effect in 1944, the UK was the superpower, and the British pound was used as the reserve currency. In the gold currency standard, a country could print their currency as much as they had gold. Since the UK was powerful, they had a lot of gold and if asked, could replace the pound for gold. Owning the pound meant own-ing gold. Based on the gold the UK was holding, the pound became the central currency of world trade. However, during

World War I and II, the gold of Europe, including the UK, flowed into the US, who provided military supplies. After World War II, as the US agreed on trading thirty-five dollars for one ounce of gold with the Bretton Woods system, the dollar became the reserve currency. In a gold currency standard, this was natural.

Then problems occurred in the 1960s. Already in the 1950s, the US continuously experienced chronic current account deficits, and later on, due to the intervention in the Vietnam War, there was a surge in spending. In the 1960s, the dollar reserves of foreign governments and the central bank exceeded the amount of gold the US had. In other words, there was not enough gold to trade for dollars. Countries began to exchange dollars into gold, and the US's gold reserves rapidly decreased. Finally, in 1971, President Richard Nixon declared that the US wouldn't exchange dollars for gold anymore. Afterward, the value of the dollar continuously decreased and the relationship between the dollar and gold was severed. Then countries worldwide started to use the floating exchange rate system. At the time, US's gold reserves were depleted trying to support the economy of Western countries and competing against the Soviet Union in the Cold War. However, the situation was different from when the UK handed the reserve currency status to the US because the Western countries could not survive without the US. So the dollar stayed as the reserve currency.

However, because the dollar was not gold, a decrease in the dollar's value could not be avoided.

Soon after, the US developed a better reserve currency system. In 1975, OPEC started taking only US dollars for oil. The demand for dollars increased when the oil price surged with the first oil shock in 1973. Since there is almost no country that could live without oil, every country needed to retain an enough amount of dollars to buy oil. When the dollar was exchangeable with gold, a demand for dollars was not needed. In other words, the dollar was only in the form of paper, but was actually gold. However, in a floating exchange rate system the dollar does not have a value of its own. If we should compare it to gold coins, the dollar is worth the amount of paper needed to create it. Therefore, the value of the paper dollar is determined by supply and demand. Since the supply is decided by the US, the important part is the demand. In other words, to keep the dollar as the reserve currency and benefit from it, the most important thing is to create demand. Oil is a necessary resource. If dollars are needed to buy oil, then the demand is ensured. The more the price of oil rises, the more demand there is for dollars; and the US can supply more dollars. If the demand of the US dollar increases, then the US can literally print more dollars. This is a privilege to the US, which is like printing gold. Other countries need to provide goods or services, and all that the US needs to do is print and supply dollars. If there is demand, there is no problem. In a gold currency standard, a currency could be printed only to the amount of gold that was brought in from other countries. Now the US can print as much as there is demand. It's like magic. This magic may come out as the rise in oil price or inflation, and thankfully inflation decreases debt. If the US or Europe have trouble due to excessive debt, a proper amount of inflation may actually help decrease debt. However, the proper amount of inflation for them may not be proper for other countries. It can be poisonous to other countries.

There is one fatal flaw to this magic, and that is disappearance of demand. If the demand for the dollar exists, it is treated like gold. However, if there is no demand for the dollar, then it is only a piece of paper. The US might have issued too many dollars in the 2000s. Figure 3-6 is the M2/GDP graph of the US, which shows how many dollars were issued compared to the real economy. We can see that the numbers have risen to the level of the 1970s when the dollar faced a crisis. As the value of the dollar continuously decreased, Iran, Iraq, and Venezuela considered, or actually traded, in different currencies. A possible alternative was the Euro; but due to a financial crisis, Europe is not in a good situation. In order to prevent the disappearance of the demand for dollars, the US has to be careful with many things. A strong alternative currency for the dollar, billing of oil by oil-producing countries with currencies other than the dollar, and oil importers agreeing enthusiastically with paying in different currencies are all not good. The disappearance of demand poses a serious threat to the reserve currency status and national power of the US. As the Lehman Brother crisis occurred in the US, the dollar was at risk of losing its reserve currency status. However, as Europe fell into a financial crisis, the Euro was in danger. The demand for dollars rapidly increased and the risk of losing its reserve currency status was gone. If the oil price rises, the demand for dollars will increase, and countries will try to secure more dollars. The importance of the dollar will increase in foreign exchange reserves, and the reserve currency status for the dollar will solidify. However, as there is more supply of dollars, this does not mean the dollar will be strong.

We have already examined the effect of the oil price and the dollar together with the ODCI. The oil price is displayed in dollars, and the in the Bretton Woods system one dollar was fixed at 1/35 ounces of gold. If we assume that the oil price per barrel is one hundred dollars, one barrel of oil is worth 100/35 ounces of gold. But as the system changed into the floating exchange rate system, the value of the dollar changed, and this affected the actual value of the oil.

We have seen that the value of the dollar sometimes doubles, and other times is cut in half, through the dollar index. We have also seen the change in the value of the dollar may act as leverage to the change in oil price and maximize the real effect of the oil shock. For example, in a floating exchange rate system, even if the oil price is one hundred dollars, it could be worth 200/35 ounces of gold or 50/35 ounces of gold. As the value of the dollar became volatile, the fluctuations in the oil price have increased.

Oil and the dollar also affect the value of each other. This is because oil and the dollar act as alternatives for each other in financial products. Usually when the dollar is weak, oil is strong; and when the dollar is strong, oil is weak. This can be seen as the result of the flow of funds in financial markets. This can also be seen as the result of inflation due to the value of the dollar dropping when too much money is released. However, the two do not always move in the opposite direction, and even if they move in the same direction, the slope can be different. Therefore, it will help to use the ODCI to understand the exact effects.

Figure 3-6. US M2/GDP (1964-2011)

Source: FRB/OECD

The Arab Spring

On December 17, 2010, a young man named Mohamed Bouazizi set his body on fire in Tunisia. This was a catalyst for the Tunisian revolution. Mohamed Bouazizi couldn't find a job, so he sold fruit in the street without a permit. One day, the police officials insulted him and confiscated his fruit cart. He went to the governor's office and complained, but was kicked out. So he decided to self-immolate. He died on January 4, 2011, eighteen days after self-immolation. The citizens' complaints of high unemployment, severe financial distress due to high inflation, and the government's corruption developed into a demonstration after this event. Tunisia's President Ben Ali fled to Saudi Arabia and the twenty-four years of dictatorship collapsed. This event was named as the Jasmine Revolution because the national flower of Tunisia is jasmine.

The anti-government protests expanded to Egypt, Algeria, Libya, Bahrain, and across the Middle East and North Africa. This is called the Arab Spring. Egypt's President Hosni Mubarak resigned in February of 2011 and the thirty years of dictatorship ended. In October of 2011, after forty-two years of Libyan dictatorship, Muammar Gaddafi died, and the eight-month civil war ended.

Other small and large anti-government protests occurred in other countries. According to ILO (International Labour Organization), one-fourth of the youth in the Middle East are unemployed. Arab countries that witnessed revolutions arising because of financial distress and high inflation increased government spending to stabilize society. Saudi Arabia gave out housing loans with no interest and increased the wages of government officials. Kuwait gave out cash free of charge. Government spending of the Arab countries is rapidly increasing.

Increase in fiscal spending to appease the public increased the budget balance oil price. A country needs to make up for increasing expenditures, due to creating jobs and supporting food and energy, by increasing the income. The oil price needed for the income to make up for the spending in national finance is the budget balance oil price. Saudi Arabia's budget balance oil price was forty-two dollars, forty-nine dollars, and fifty-four dollars from 2009 to 2011, but surged to eighty dollars in 2012. The budget balance oil price soaring due to high inflation and expansion of fiscal spending served as an increase in the lowest point of oil price. When the oil price dropped from $140 to thirty dollars with the Lehman Brothers crisis in 2008, the oil price did not stay long under the budget balance oil price of Saudi Arabia and rose again. On the other hand, when the budget balance oil price was at the forty-dollar level the oil price soared to $140. As Saudi Arabia's budget balance oil price was eighty dollars as of 2012, and considering that this is the lowest point, the highest point of oil price can even be slightly below three hundred dollars. Of course, in the next few years, Saudi Arabia's budget balance oil price will most likely exceed one hundred dollars, and some OPEC countries and Russia already need a higher budget balance oil price.

If the budget balance oil price of Saudi Arabia and other OPEC countries rise, will the oil price also go up? Probably so! There is still more than 70 percent of worldwide oil reserves buried under the territory of OPEC countries. Saudi Arabia still affects the demand and supply of worldwide oil. If the oil price falls beneath the budget balance oil price, the OPEC countries will have more expenditures than income. Then the OPEC countries will need to cut back on expenditures for social stability, but this is not an option since the Arab Spring occurred. OPEC countries will rather cut production to increase the oil price and increase export revenues. The US needs to take OPEC's position into consideration if they want to keep the billing currency for oil to stay as the dollar.

What would be the worst-case scenario for the US? That would be OPEC cooperating with China. China would secure energy and OPEC would secure a rising market. Furthermore, if OPEC changed the billing currency from the dollar to China's Yuan, the demand for dollars would rapidly decrease and threaten the reserve currency status. Countries will sell dollars to secure Yuan. This fits with China's strategy of international-ization of the Yuan. China will suddenly rise as a superpower in commodities and financial markets, and the US dollar will lose its power. To avoid this situation, OPEC needs to be satisfied with the current system; easily said, OPEC needs to be financially well-off. Just as the US helped Europe with the Marshall Plan after World War II, a Marshall Plan for the Middle East may be needed. Since Europe did not produce oil, dollars were poured in. In the case of the Middle East, one method would be is to raise the oil price. The Middle East needs to be financially well-off so that they are satisfied with their current partners, and so that they stay away from alternatives like China.

Redistribution of Global Wealth

In 2000, the US currency compared to the real economy sharply increased (Figure 3-6). The extremely low interest rate that lasted over a long period of time after year 2000 probably played the biggest role in rapidly increasing the M2/GDP. After 2000, the long lasted extremely low interest rate (Figure 2-4) of the US created asset bubbles. The collapse of these asset bubbles led to the Lehman Brothers crisis. Asset prices plummeted as the bubbles collapsed. This crisis was blocked by providing liquidity, in other words, releasing more money. The US may have privileges having the reserve currency, but looking at recent events of Europe, inflation is to be expected. At first Europe tried to overcome the debt crisis with a retrenchment policy. But as the policy brought financial distress and didn't work so well, after the 2012 France president elections, Europe is trying to solve the problem with economic growth. In other words, instead of harsh restructuring through retrenchment, Europe is releasing money to relax the immediate economic pain. The US and IMF are also suggesting to Europe a growth solution instead of a retrenchment policy as an answer to the debt crisis. Also, Brazil and Australia have decreased interest rates and are now focusing on stimulating the economy through growth. Of course, growth may be a good answer to the problem. However, when the economy gets better, it will be hard to avoid inflation. Easily said, there will most likely be side effects to solving the aftereffects of the bubble, which was created with the increase in money, with money.

If an inflation problem occurs, the US and Europe, because of their debt, will relatively decrease in debt. Additionally, countries with a lot of natural resources, like Russia, Brazil, and Australia, not to mention OPEC countries, will be in a favorable position if inflation occurs. On the other hand, China, which has a lot of cash and is increasing dependency on oil, will not be in a favorable position. High inflation can have China's Yuan revalued upward, and although this will increase China's purchasing power, it will decrease export competitiveness. Attempts of internationalizing China's Yuan, combined with growing openness, China's financial market will continuously expose weaknesses, and an oil shock followed by a dollar shock may occur. And this will be accompanied by the movement of global wealth from China to the developed countries. Of course, China's crisis will most likely spread to other Asian and third-world countries, and considering lessons from the past, preparations are required for even a dollar shock.

What would be the causes of the third oil shock? Reasons commonly suggested, such as a conflict in a certain country or a single event will probably not precipitate another oil shock. A specific issue may be pointed out, but the root cause of the third oil shock will most likely be the manifestation of the interest of global forces. It is as if Mohamed Bouazizi can be the symbol for Arab Spring, but cannot be the root cause for it. That is, the third oil shock may occur with the shift in the balance of global power. It seems such an environment is building up, and it also seems it will not take too long to see the accumulated problems erupt above the surface.

Conclusions

A situation is building up for the third oil shock to likely occur, and this might be accompanied by a dollar shock. History repeats itself.

Appendix: Recent shale gas development and energy independence of China

China Trying to Find a Breakthrough with Shale Gas

Preview

Currently, China is a major energy-importing country. So, they are vulnerable to fluctuations in energy price. The future will be the same. Shale gas will be a determining factor for China's future.

Summary

China is taking interest in what is recently called the biggest revolution in the energy industry, shale gas. They are trying to develop shale gas, which they have an abundance of in reserves, to become a natural gas-producing country. Additionally, China is constructing a variety of petrochemical facilities that use gas as raw material. Moreover, China is borrowing the latest technology that converts gas into oil, and is trying to excel in the field of energy.

Shale Gas is Becoming Popular

It's not that China is not rich in natural resources, but they don't have the infrastructure to collect these resources. And considering China's population and growth rate, they need to import energy. Unfortunately, China's natural resources for energy are mostly coal. Compared to that, they don't have an abundance of oil and conventional natural gas, so they need to continuously import these fossil fuels. Therefore, they are vulnerable to external shocks (for example, a sharp rise in the oil price).

EIA recently announced that China has a mass amount of natural gas (shale gas). The size of the reserves is approximately forty-five trillion cubic meters (m^3). It may be hard to imagine how much this is. This is the amount of running one hundred units of a 1.2GW nuclear power plant for 260 years.

Worldwide energy institutions are interested and watching what China will do. The biggest issue right now is whether China will become an energy independent country by developing shale gas on a large scale with the US.

If China becomes an energy independent country, they can decrease their dependence on oil. Of course, oil is not used only for energy. Rather, it is more used for petrochemical products and transportation. However, recent advances in technology have enabled commercialization of GTL (gas to liquid) technologies, which can change gas to oil, such as diesel. Therefore, if gas can be collected in abundance, petroleum liquid fuels, such as diesel and naphtha, can be secured through investment in infrastructure.

Will China be able to convert to an energy independent country through the development of shale gas? China's natural gas reserve is 2.5 trillion m^3, but shale gas reserve is forty-five trillion m^3. If an abundant amount of shale gas is produced, and if the gas is converted into petroleum (usually diesel) with the GTL technology, China will not only become an energy independent country, but can also become a net exporter. However, it is still too early, and there are still many obstacles to overcome for China to see this come to a realization.

Reasons Why Shale Gas is Becoming Popular

Natural gas is divided into associated gas and non-associated gas. These two put together are called conventional gas. In other words, this is the conventional form in which we collect gas. If there is conventional gas, there should also be unconventional gas. The gas that is recently attracting attention, shale gas, is an unconventional gas. Unconventional gas is gas that is not buried in oilfields or gas fields but is buried in strata, bedrock, or oil sands.

Then why is it that unconventional gas is suddenly receiving attention? The answer lies in the development of extraction technology. First, conventional gas obviously had the advantage of being easy to extract. Because conventional gas is concentrated in a small area, all you needed to do is set a drilling rig and extract oil. However, unconventional gas, such as shale gas, is usually spread across a large area, which makes extraction costs high. Thus, until the 2000s, people were not interested in unconventional gas. Rather, people got interested in the environment, criticized the existing carbon-centered economy, and started developing renewable energy, such as solar and wind power. Meanwhile, led by the US, economically viable extraction technology of unconventional gas was developed. Compared to the traditional vertical drilling, a much more economically cheap horizontal drilling was developed.

With the traditional vertical drilling, gas that was widespread was hard to extract. It was economically infeasible to set a number of boreholes over a wide area. Since shale gas was not buried narrow and deep, but wide and thin, it was economically infeasible in the first place with vertical drilling. However, the US developed the horizontal drilling, which is fit for drilling wide areas. Horizontal drilling is a technology that puts a pipe vertically two to four kilometers underground (up to this point, it's the same with vertical drilling), then bends the pipe horizontally; this makes it fit for extracting resources that are buried wide and thin underground, like shale gas. In the vertical process, a borehole is needed every fifty meters. However, in the horizontal process, only one borehole is needed for four hundred. This way, the US could access energy resources that were not possible to reach in the past.

As the horizontal drilling technology was developed in 2001, the US's natural gas production started to increase. By 2005, extraction of unconventional gas surpassed conventional gas. By 2008, conventional gas was approximately four billion m^3 and unconventional gas production was approximately forty-five billion m^3 (more than ten times conventional gas). Currently, the US's shale gas reserve is known to be approximately forty-five trillion m^3, and worldwide unconventional gas reserve is predicted to be more than two hundred trillion m^3. Henceforth, shale gas will be available worldwide through horizontal drilling technologies. This is the so-called "Shale Gas Revolution." Two hundred trillion m^3 is an enormous amount which is the same amount as conventional gas is buried worldwide. Thanks to the full-fledged development of shale gas in the 2000s, the US has gained the possibility of converting from an energy import country to an energy export country. This possibility became reality in 2012.

In February of 2012, the US signed a natural gas export agreement with India. The world was shocked when they heard that the US was going to export gas to India, because in the 1990s, the US created ten terminals to import gas. The export of US's natural gas brought an enormous impact, and definitely imprinted the existence of shale gas to the world. Currently, the US has already gotten export approval for approximately sixty million tons of LNG, out of one hundred million tons of LNG that will be available through nine shale gas development projects. They are also awaiting export approval for the remaining forty million tons of LNG. Of course, such energy export policies are strategic in that it only applies to countries that have signed the FTA with the US But from a larger standpoint, we must note that the emergence of shale gas has made an energy import country like the US into an energy independent country, and moreover, into an energy export country.

There is also considerable amount of shale gas in China. According to EIA, there is approximately forty-five trillion m^3 of shale gas buried. So China is trying to react quickly. The Chinese government has started to explore shale gas with foreign companies that can develop shale gas. Shell and CNPC has agreed on developing shale gas in Sichuan together, and BP and SINOPEC are exploring for shale gas together as well. In 2011, CNOOC invested $570 million in Chesapeake, and such energy developments are continuing. In 2010, the Chinese government ordered national energy companies to be able to produce 37 percent of natural gas consumption with shale gas. Such movements are expected continue into the future. China has always wanted to become an energy independent country because, as an energy import country, the economy is vulnerable to drastic changes in energy price. Shale gas is recognized to be China's answer to these structural problems.

Return of the Carbon Economy

In the early 2000s, renewable energy, such as wind, solar, and geothermal, was in the limelight. At the same time, companies that were in the business of renewable energy came into the spotlight. If solar energy was suggested to be part of business in the annual report, the stock price would rise. Companies that manufactured wind turbines and related equipment were recognized as the leading group that would dominate the future energy market. It seemed as if the carbon oriented economy, which brought high growth in the past, was about to disappear into the past with the criticism of environmental destruction.

However, unfortunately, renewable energy is not the energy for the near future. According to ExxonMobil's report on energy forecast (*2012 The Outlook for Energy: A View to 2040*), in 2040, renewable energy (mostly water and wind) will only take up 7 percent of worldwide energy sources. Traditional energy sources—crude oil, coal, and gas—will still be responsible for 80 percent of total energy demand. In fact, it is hard to find a company that is making healthy profits in the renewable energy industry. Rather, the oil majors and oil-producing countries' hegemony of carbon have grown stronger. It is once again the era of carbon.

In particular, natural gas is being further highlighted. Compared to coal, natural gas not only emits 60 percent less carbon dioxide (CO_2), but also less sulfur oxides (SO_x) and nitrogen oxides (NO_x); therefore, it is treated as well as renewable energy. It is popular for much less environment destruction. Nuclear power was the only energy source that could compete economically with natural gas. However, as the Fukushima Nuclear Accident (2011 East Japan earthquake) occurred, the safety of nuclear plants and the environmental costs of burying nuclear waste came into question. Criticisms were generated on the basis that the costs could be much higher. So it seems that it will be hard for nuclear power to procure investments for a while.

Other than the fact that natural gas is eco-friendly, the low price makes it a very attractive energy source. The Henry Hub natural gas price (the standard gas price for US) was $6.95 in 2007, rose to $8.85 in 2008, then dropped to $3.89 in 2009, $4.39 in 2010, and dropped to around $2.50 in 2012. These changes were led by shale gas.

The US is already utilizing natural gas with lowered prices. They increased the portion of natural gas for power-generating feedstock. The US is rapidly shifting the energy source for power from coal centered to gas centered. The proportion of the development of coal in the past was 55 percent, and is now only around 40 percent. In the case of natural gas, it was 20 percent in the past, but is now around 40 percent. Moreover, the gas power plants have advanced in technology. The power plants that once used a simple cycle now use a combined cycle, which is more efficient. The quality of turbines, boilers, and other major equipment for a combined cycle plant has also gotten better. Now, a natural gas combined cycle plant is not only cheaper in material costs, but also in construction costs, operating costs, and all other costs than a coal-fired power plant.

This progress is not only occurring in the US. Oil-producing countries of the Middle East that create fuel oil with abundant oil reserves and refining facilities are also quickly following. Most power plants that were constructed in the past were steam power plants that used crude oil. Except countries that had abundant gas, such as Qatar and Algeria, Middle East countries (Saudi Arabia, Kuwait, United Arab Emirates, Iran, and Iraq) ran steam power plants that used fuel oil to supply power. However, in terms of raw material of these power plants, changes occurred after 2007. As the gas price dropped to the point where replacing the oil-fired power plants were profitable, most Middle East oil-producing countries began considering gas as raw material for power. In fact, the oil-producing countries have started building gas-fired combined cycle power plants after 2010.

How Cheap is Gas? The Answer is in Energy Parity

With some physics calculations, we can know which is more economic between gas and oil. One kg of oil produces 10,700 kcal. Crude oil is traded in barrels (159 liters). One barrel is approximately 132 kg. By multiplying the two, burning one barrel of crude oil produces approximately 1,361,040 kcal. How much natural gas would we need to create the same calories?

In the case of gas, it is traded in one million BTU (British Thermal Unit), usually identified as MMBtu. 1 MMBtu has the value of 252,000 kcal. If we divide what one barrel of oil produces (1,361,040 kcal) by 252,000 kcal, we get approximately 5.4. We need about 5.4 MMBtu gas. In other words, in terms of energy parity, one barrel of oil is about 5.4 MMBtu of gas. This number is important in terms of energy.

Then what about the price? Is one barrel of oil being sold at 5.4 times the price of gas? Dubai crude is about one hundred dollars, and West Texas Intermediate (WTI) is about eighty dollars. Whereas, according to US's Henry Hub, gas is being traded at about $2.50. If we divide the price of one barrel by the price of one MMBtu gas, we get about thirty to forty. Oil is approximately thirty to forty times more expensive.

This gives important implications. In terms of purely power generation, natural gas is advantageous compared to crude oil as a feedstock. Of course, as seen above, US's shale gas played an important role in the sharply decreased natural gas price. As the supply of gas became smooth, the price dropped. Therefore, whether to use expensive oil as the source of energy or cheap gas as the source of energy is quite clear. Gas is the way to go.

Can China become an Oil-Producing Country?

As both the supply of conventional gas and unconventional gas is abundant, the focus is on the FT (Fisher-Tropsch) process. Easily explained, the FT process is the process of changing gas into fuel oil, such as diesel and naphtha. This was developed in the 1920s.

The reason why the FT process is gaining interest is because of the structure. Since the FT process is changing gas into oil, the lower the price of gas (source) and the higher the price of oil (product), the more economical it becomes. In terms of energy parity suggested above, plants that currently use the FT process can achieve high economic efficiency. In China's stance, the most wanted type of plant would be Qatar's Pearl GTL, a GTL plant. If China builds a GTL plant, they will gain the possibility of not only becoming a gas-producing country, but also a crude oil-producing country. How fantastic would this be for China?

In November 2011, Shell completed the Pearl GTL project in Qatar, which produces 260,000 bpd (barrels per day) of oil. Pearl GTL uses approximately 1.6 billion cfd (cubic feet per day) of natural gas and produces 140,000 barrels of diesel and naphtha and 120,000 barrels of gas condensates. Therefore, China has special feelings for a GTL plant. A GTL plant that uses the FT process can solve China's vulnerable energy security.

However, the economic feasibility of the GTL plant will soon be in question. Pearl GTL of Qatar uses about twelve million tons of natural gas. Is it more economical to sell this with the GTL instead of selling in the form of LNG? LNG is already linked to the expensive oil price (the international LNG price is decided according to the oil price). Even without using GTL and changing it to crude oil, LNG benefits from the increased oil price. When selling gas as gas, because the price of gas is linked to the price of crude oil, you don't really need to change it into crude oil.

Additionally, Shell announced that they used approximately nineteen billion dollars to install the GTL plant, but it only produces 260,000 barrels per day. But it only takes \$6.5 billion to construct a refinery of the same capacity. If nineteen billion dollars is about to be invested, the investor has to choose between a new oil refinery that produces about 750,000 bpd or a GTL plant that produces about 260,000 bpd. If the price of gas rises, the problem for the GTL plant becomes bigger. There is that much more risk.

GTL's precondition is China's development of shale gas. Therefore, to examine whether the development of shale gas is feasible or not, is more important.

Shale Gas is not on China's Side

Terrain that is favorable to shale gas drilling is easy to understand, even for the general public. Areas with fragile rocks, excellent porosity, permeable areas, a lot of gas in the pores, and areas that can be naturally fractured are good conditions.

The Barnett Shale in Texas, whose development of shale gas is in full swing, has a breakeven point of $3.7/MMBtu, but the Marcellus Shale has a breakeven point of $3.25/MMBtu. This is because the area of Marcellus is a stratum easier to break than the area of Barnett. It costs less to create a borehole, and it is easier to fracture. In addition, the layer of shale is closer to the surface. Thus, it is in a favorable business position because it is in a good condition for extraction.

Another key element to the development of shale gas is the pipeline infrastructure. Texas and the Great Lakes, with their abundance of shale gas, already have a pipeline transportation infrastructure that was created in the past for other natural gases. Additional pipelines don't need to be installed. The US also already has an abundant water resource infrastructure to support development of shale gas. It seems like the gods chose the US to develop shale gas.

These two points are the difference between the US and China. China's shale gas reserve is approximately forty-five trillion m^3, but the average depth is about four to six kilometers; this is deeper than US's average of two to four kilometers. Even with only this fact, the price of extraction rises. The second problem is that most of the shale gas is buried in the west part of China. There is almost no pipeline infrastructure in the west part of China. Even if it were extracted, how would they transport it? Development and transportation of shale gas may not be impossible. But for China to become a gas exporting country, it would need to install the world's largest pipeline infrastructure to connect the western and eastern parts of the country.

And most importantly, before China's shale gas development receives a boost, the price of gas will most likely rise. Even currently in the US, the price of shale gas is about $2.50, below the extraction cost of about $3.50. In other words, since the cost is higher than the sales price, if a company cannot achieve economies of scale, they will run out of business. Medium-sized companies are gradually withdrawing from shale gas business. Therefore, in the next two to three years, major companies will most likely acquire or merge with mid-sized companies. Thus, the price of natural gas in the US is slowly rising. Who could afford to continue a business that costs more than it makes?

This comes as more deadly to China. China doesn't have the infrastructure set up like the US, and the extraction environment is not as good. In the US, where both conditions are better, the cost of production is about $3.50. How much would it be in China? Of course, China has much lower labor costs. However, the development of shale gas is done by equipment, not people. Considering the pipeline infrastructure that needs to be installed, the equipment, and the environment, will China be able to develop shale gas up to the point that it is meaningful? And will China be able to use the extracted gas to fulfill increasing energy demand? Furthermore, will they be able to reach the status of an oil-producing country using technology such as GTL?

In the past, developed countries steadily invested about 10 percent of their GDP for several decades to build infrastructure for economic growth. The US, with its large investments, has been able to pick the fruit of shale gas. However, for an emerging country like China, such investments are too big of a financial burden. Even if the investments were made, and gas extraction was possible, they could not be sure whether the price would be competitive compared to the conventional gas that Qatar, Algeria, and Australia produce. In the early twenty-first century, interest in renewable energy greatly increased and investment were active. However, humanity learned in the end that the cost of developing renewable energy was higher than the existing development of crude oil, coal, and gas. China's gas price will be so high (from massive investment in infrastructure and the overcoming of poor gas extraction environment) that it will naturally die out (like the renewable energy of the twenty-first century).

Therefore, China will develop shale gas for a while, but will not be able to do a large-scale development that could meet energy demands. In other words, China will remain as an energy importing country. If China's economy structure, an energy importing country, does not change, it will stay vulnerable to the oil price and gas price. Since China doesn't have enough oil, and since oil is important in development, China will try to change gas into oil with GTL. However, this last card will become obsolete. Therefore, China will never be free from an oil shock.

Notes

1. Sejune Oh, Why Dollar is stronger than America (One & one books, 2012)
2. Heesoo Lee, Islam (Cheong-A books, 2011)
3. Chris Harman, Class struggles in Eastern Europe 1945-83 (MW books 1988)
4. Charles P. Kindleberger, Manias, Panics, and Crashes: A History of Financial Crises (Wiley, 2005)
5. Valerie Marcel, John V. Mitchell, Oil Titans (Brookings Institution Press, 2006)
6. Nathan Lewis, Gold: The once and future money (Wiley, 2007)
7. Günter Barudio, Tränen des Teufels. Die Weltgeschichte des Erdöl (Klett-Cotta, 2001)
8. Leonardo Maugeri, The Age of Oil: What they don't want you to know about the world's most controversial resources (The Lyons Press, 2007)

9. James R. Norman, The Oil Card: Global economic warfare in the 21st century (Trine Day, 2008)

10. Anthony Sampson, The Seven Sisters: The great oil companies & the world they shaped (Viking Adult, 1975)

11. F. William Engdahl, A Century of War: Anglo-American oil politics and the new world order (Edition. Engdahl, 2011)

12. Ellen Hodgson Brown, Web of Debt: The shocking truth about our money system and how we can break free (Third millennium press, 2012)

13. Barry Eichengreen, Exorbitant Privilege: The rise and fall of the dollar and the future of the international monetary system (Oxford University Press, 2012)

14. Jeffery Robinson, Yamani: The inside story (HarperCollins Publishers, 1989)

15. www.iea.org

16. www.eia.gov

17. www.bp.com

18. www.opec.org

19. www.worldbank.org

20. www.imf.org

www.ingramcontent.com/pod-product-compliance
Lightning Source LLC
Chambersburg PA
CBHW061508180526
45171CB00001B/89